excavating history

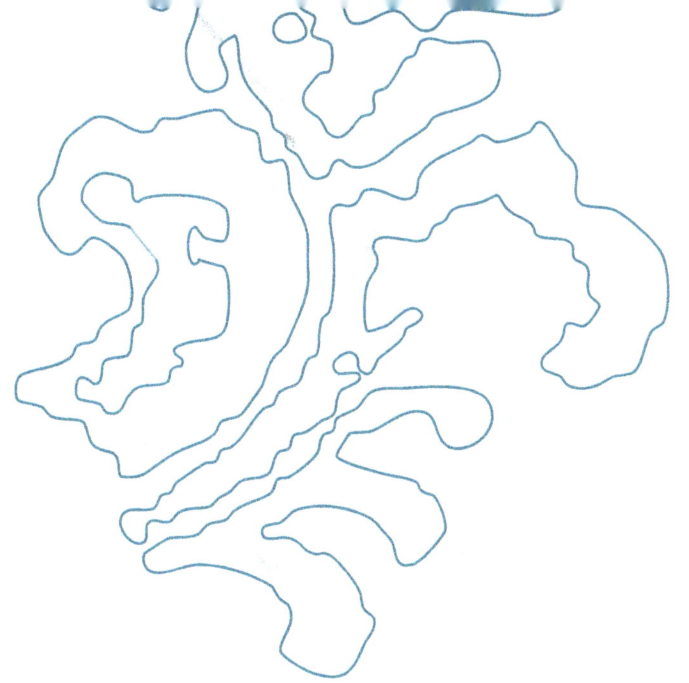

excavating history

artists take on historic sites

rebecca keller

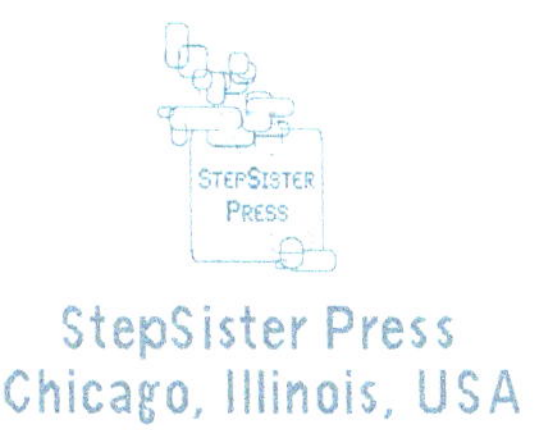

StepSister Press
Chicago, Illinois, USA

cover and interior design by Annie Heckman
copy editing Jacqueline U. Heckman

note backgrounds Maral Hashemi, Annie Heckman, Briana Schweizer
design elements from wallpaper at Jane Addams Hull-House Museum
images from Géricault, Leutze, Taft in the public domain
photograph by Arthur Rothstein, Library of Congress archives
images and text used with kind permission from copyright holders
special thanks to Gilly Youner (twitter: @gillyarcht) for her photographic contribution, page 168

ISBN: 978-0-9802300-5-5
First edition released January 2012
Second printing August 2015

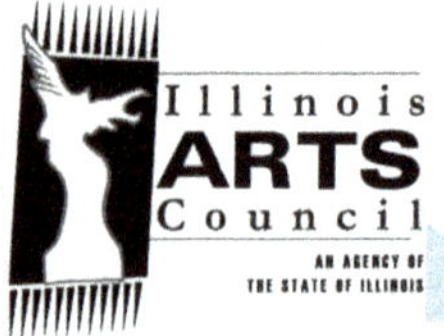

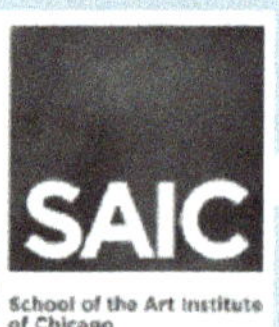

This project is partially supported by a grant from the Illinois Arts Council, a state agency. We gratefully acknowledge support from the School of the Art Institute of Chicago. We thank these organizations and all contributing artists and writers for their generous support. Without their enthusiastic contributions of time and funds, this project would not have been possible. Please link directly to these artists and organizations when sharing news about their work in this book in order to continue supporting their practices.

published by StepSister Press
StepSister Press, LLC
600 S. Crescent Avenue, Park Ridge, IL, USA
stepsisterpress.org

To excavators everywhere.

Mysteries: [illegible]

The tenth [illegible]

[illegible]

and the [illegible]

called the [illegible]

Orphic [illegible]

[illegible]

giving principle [illegible]

of life [illegible]

means "pertaining [illegible]

from the Greek [illegible]

Therefore the [illegible]

an internal [illegible]

contents

acknowledgments 11

history and the artistic imagination 15
rebecca keller

about excavating history 27
rebecca keller

excavating: three years, three sites 57
rebecca keller

(1) excavating the pleasant home 2008...61
rebecca keller

home for the histories 67
vince michael

(2) excavating the loop 2009 71
rebecca keller

why excavate histories? 79
mary jane jacob

(3) excavating hull-house 2010 83

welcoming museum takeovers (or, what to expect when you're expecting the unexpected)..... 91
lisa junkin

a proliferation of metaphor and artmaking like baseball................................ 113
rebecca keller

alumni essays

chiara galimberti 123

elise goldstein 127

briana schweizer 131

amber ginsburg 137

letter to a collective 143
EXPECTING YOU WITH PLEASURE (LOVE)
annie heckman

an excavating history guidebook 161
rebecca keller

contributor biographies 175

acknowledgments

Many thanks to the artists, students, curators, educators, historians, activists, and writers who made these projects possible: Anne Parmasto and Raili Marling of the University of Tartu; Laura Thompson at the Pleasant Home; Nathan Mason at the Chicago Cultural Center; Lisa Lee, Lisa Junkin, Michael Plummer and the Hull-House Museum staff; Lindsey Thieman and Jack Whalen of the International Museum of Surgical Science; my colleagues at the School of the Art Institute of Chicago, and Annie Heckman and StepSister Press for the beautiful book.

Deep thanks to Simone and Isabel for patience with their busy mother, and deepest thanks to my husband Mark, for his intelligence, support, and encouragement.

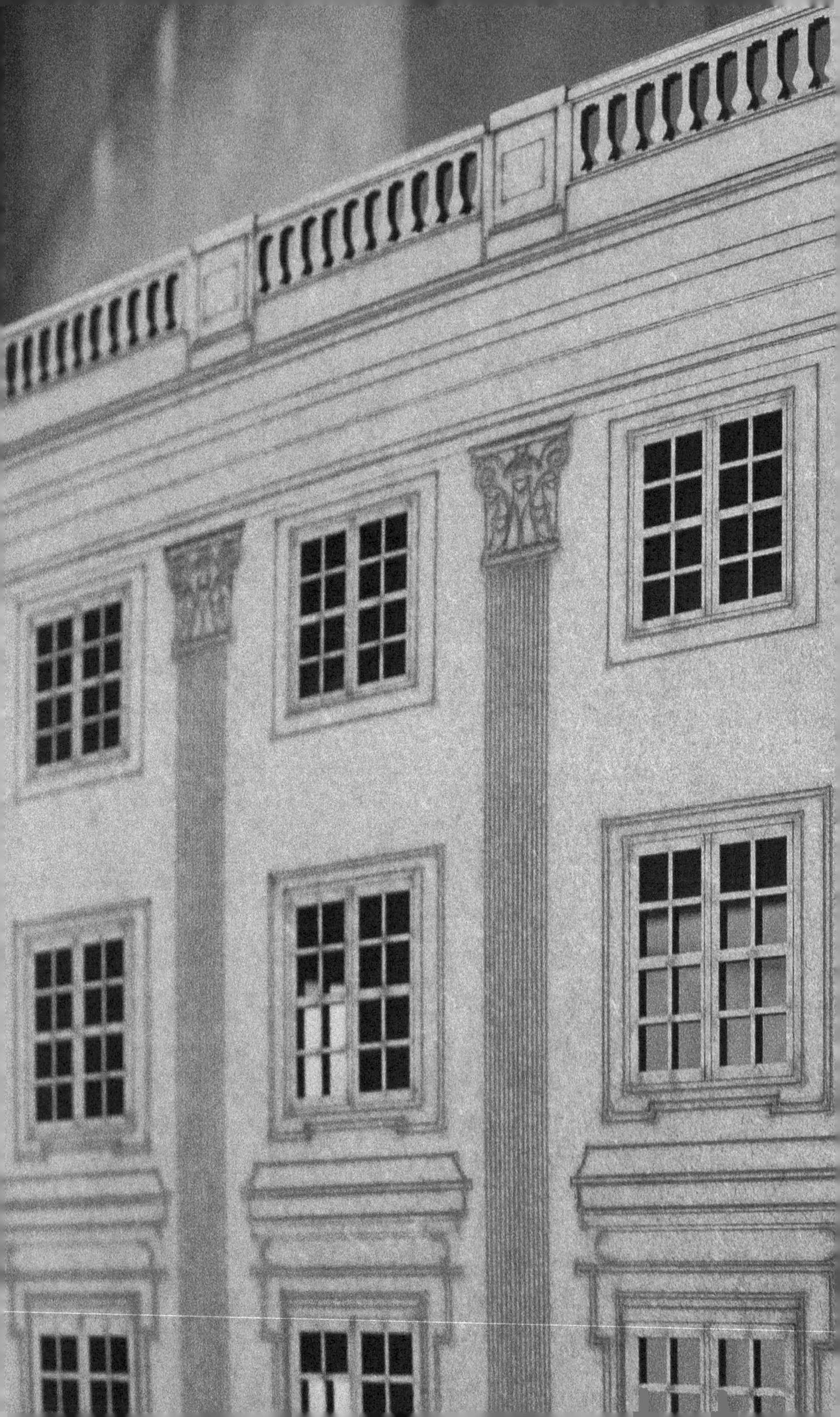

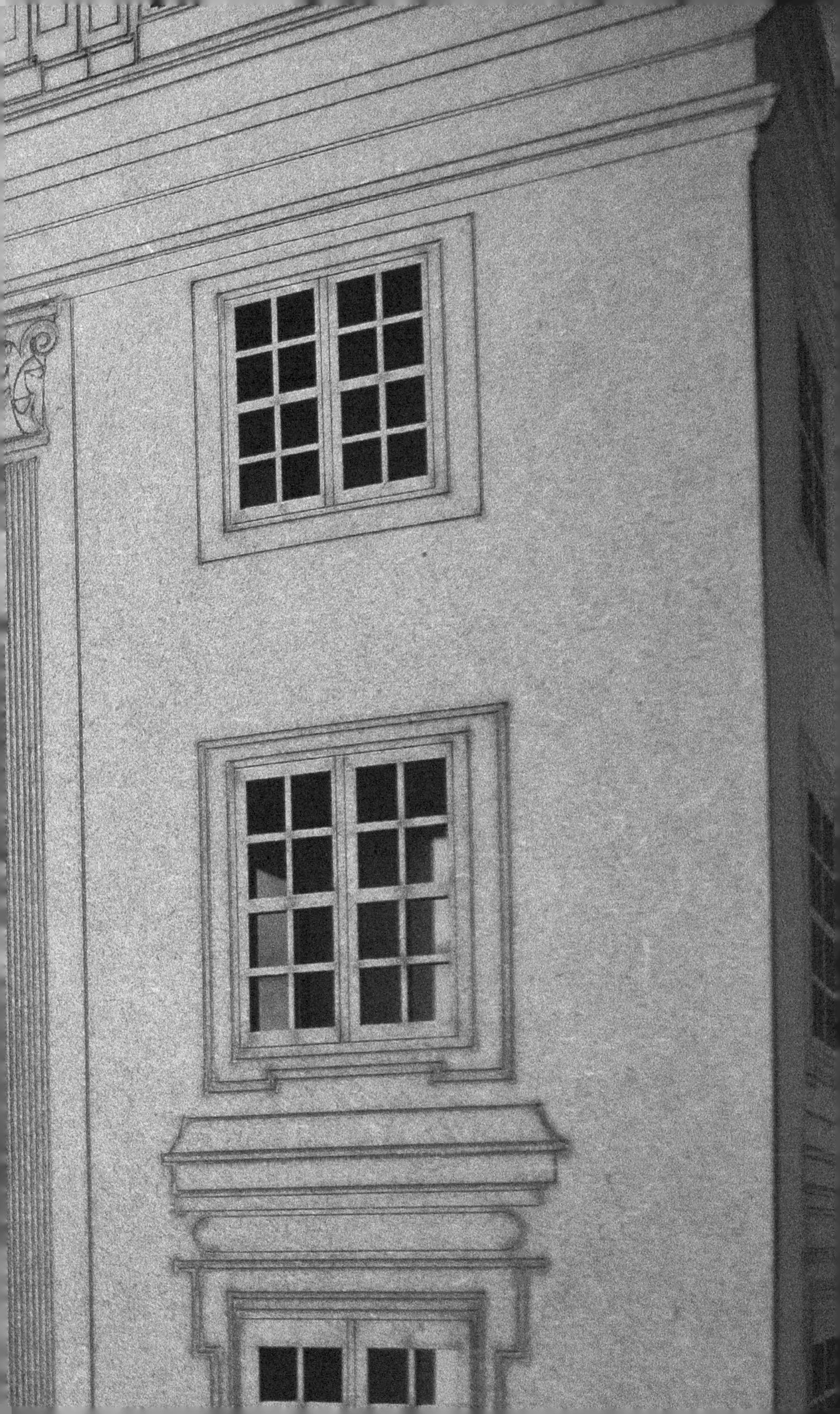

[illegible]

O negative [illegible] ([illegible])

d type universal donor)

n of gift giving (messianic)

ved my father, I must

something back (in and

myself) Don't know what

to do, can't say thank you

.

blood drawn

t thread from Korea, (where

probably from" surname

s Korea, not China because

o, not r

merchants visited "Goryeo" in

ughout 13th century (look-up)

e thread (with blood)" The

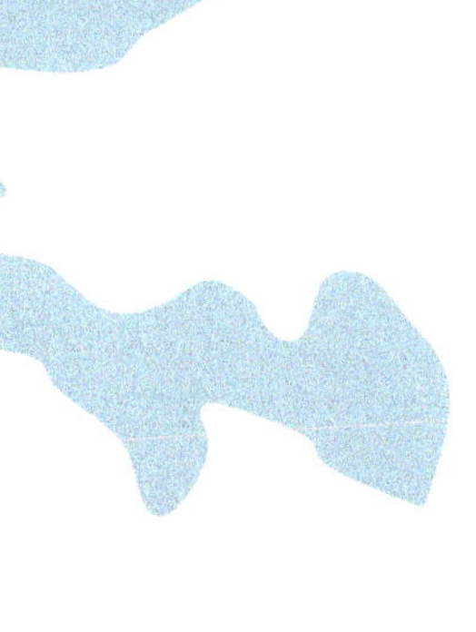

history and the artistic imagination

rebecca keller

truth claims and unreliable narratives

In the "hierarchy of genres" proposed by the historian André Félibien and accepted by art academies throughout Europe, history painting was at the top of the heap—the most noble pursuit in art. Moreover, as Félibien defined it, history painting did not limit itself to actual history. Mythological or allegorical subjects served as well. The point was to create a grand heroic narrative. The point was to convey a higher truth, unencumbered by mere fact.

For instance, thanks to Emanuel Leutze's painting, *Washington Crossing the Delaware,* any school kid can tell you what George

previous spread: Liene Bosquê, *Eleanor Robinson Countiss' Petit Home,* 2011, laser cut on MDF, 22 x 9.5 x 18.5 inches *photo Annie Heckman*

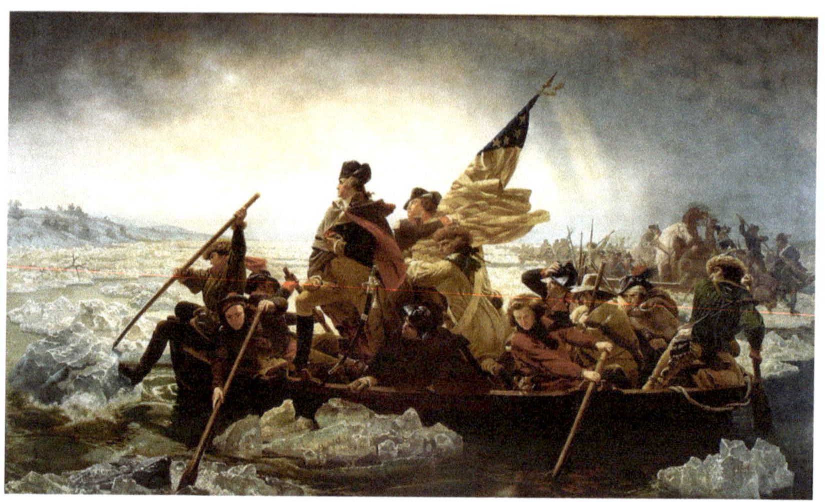

Emanuel Leutze, *Washington Crossing the Delaware*, 1851
oil on canvas, 12 feet 5 inches x 21 feet 3 inches

Washington looked like during the battle of Trenton, just as, thanks to Théodore Géricault's great work (p. 19), we know that the survivors of the shipwrecked frigate Medusa could writhe energetically despite starvation and exposure.

There is easy sport in picking out the inaccuracies in Leutze's *Washington Crossing the Delaware:* the flag flying in the painting hadn't been designed when the event actually happened, for example. Today, it may be mainly sticklers for accuracy who know—or care—that Washington's ragtag army crossed the river in the middle of the night during a fierce storm, rather than emerging from the dewy mist into a bright sunlit future of freedom, as Leutze portrays.

The moment that Leutze depicted is generally believed to be the turning point in the American Revolutionary War. On that Christmas night of 1776, Washington was convinced that the British were about to cross the river and drive the Americans back to Philadelphia. Action was urgent. He was somehow able to motivate a starving and ragtag force to cross a stormy, ice-choked river in the middle of the night in order to attack the amassed army of one of the world's superpowers. The British and Hessian troops were taken by surprise, and the rest, as they say, is history. But it could have ended much differently, and doubtless Washington himself knew just how much he risked in those flimsy boats. This real story is more dramatic, and less trite, than the version Leutze gives us, which looks like it could be subtitled, "George Washington Sails Confidently into the Sunrise of Liberty."

Here is the double bind of the artist working with historical material. We make things known by making them visible: the more powerful the visual form, the more memorable it is. Yet anyone making a work of art edits, emphasizes, deletes. These images are not peer-reviewed for accuracy. Artists are free to prefer interesting apocrypha, a compelling image, or a persuasive story to the complications of factual narrative. They might feel historic events are a starting point rather than something they have a duty towards. And because it is art, not history, artists can ask the historians and fact-checkers to hold their coats while they roll up their sleeves and get to work, work that might contain imagined events or editorializing or sheer invention. In fiction they might be called "unreliable narrators." In art-making, the question doesn't get asked all that much.

With history painting such as Leutze's, certain assumptions are also at play, assumptions about the relative importance of the event being depicted and about the commonality of the cultural currency. A mere seventy-five years separates the creation of Leutze's painting from Washington's famous victory. Leutze could have assumed that the details of such a famous event—details that were well-documented and widely agreed upon—would be remembered. His job as the artist was to present the higher, symbolic truth: the sun is behind Washington, illuminating the good General as he emerges out of the storm to the dawn of victory. It would be interesting to survey whether or not this relationship has now been turned on its head: I suspect that nowadays people are more familiar with the painting, and therefore with Leutze's version of the story, than with the reality he based it on.

There are several histories in every depiction of history: the moment depicted is obvious, but what about the moment the work of art is made? The context of the historical present is partly what influences an artist to select a subject. Leutze painted his famous work in Düsseldorf in 1851. Shortly before, Germany had experienced revolutions that sought to create a national parliament out of 38 loosely confederated German states. As Leutze made the painting, Germany was engaged, like much of Europe, with revolutionary hopes, born of the Enlightenment and fed by the inspirational aspects of the American Revolution. There is an invisible irony here: The forces that were defeated by Washington's Colonial Army included 1500 Hessian troops, German mercenaries fighting for the British. According to an 1880 *New York Times* article on the mercenaries, at the time of the American Revolution, German opinion was extremely pro-British. Thus Leutze's admiring portrait of Washington reflects changing German cultural attitudes as much as it portrays the events on the Delaware. Leutze was responding to a European audience hungry for heroic David-and-Goliath tales of freedom fighters winning against great odds. Perhaps the colonial army's heroism in 1776 served as the perfect screen upon which Leutze was able to project the important struggles of his time, his culture.

Géricault's *The Raft of the Medusa* is another example of history painting, but in one sense it is not history painting at all, because the event and the artwork happened at roughly the same time.

In 1816, the French frigate Medusa was sent to take possession of the Senegalese port of St.Louis, a gift from England to the newly restored French monarchy. The incompetent but politically well-connected captain wrecked the ship. Officers and assorted grandees took the lifeboats, leaving the 150 crewmen on a half-sinking raft, where desperation led to murder and cannibalism. The ordeal ended when one of the other ships in the convoy accidentally came upon the raft and found a few survivors still alive amongst the decomposing bodies. They were returned to France, and a scandal unfolded.

Géricault became obsessed with the story, and made the then unheard-of decision to depict anonymous people and a contemporary event in the style of grand history painting, without a commission. He interviewed survivors, made sketches, even studied dismembered cadavers in his studio. The huge painting (almost 16 x 23 feet) provided a focus for the outrage, and

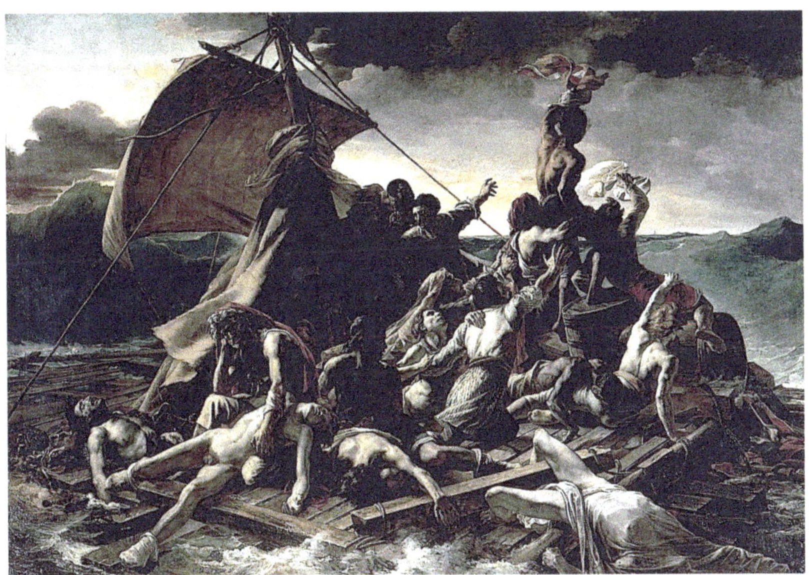

Théodore Géricault, *The Raft of the Medusa*, 1818–1819
oil on canvas, 16 feet x 23 feet 5 inches

offered a singular vision to capture and amplify the emotion. Géricault used the conventions of history painting—enormous size, powerful composition, a sense of spectacle—to draw attention to an event that official France wanted to ignore.

So, should we care that Géricault's sailors are muscular instead of emaciated? That the men on the raft look as if they are cooperating rather than murdering one another? Of course not. But perhaps we should care that the discussion of this painting so often stops at emphasizing composition and formal analysis, or cites it as an example of the common theme in Romanticism of "man against nature"? This painting strikes me as a deeply political act, and one that required enormous effort on Géricault's part. He died at the age of only thirty-three, just two years after finishing it.

Would anyone ever think about what happened on the Medusa if it were not for Géricault? When an artist chooses to tell such a story, he or she lays down a marker and creates a trail for the curious or outraged to follow. Artists are not necessarily documentarians, but they are citizens. They are free to dwell in apocrypha and myth. What they are getting at is emotional, cultural truth.

history as future

When the context of an image or work of art changes, the work of art is open to being re-interpreted or re-engaged. I often show my students a 1936 photograph byArthur Rothstein. It is a black-and-white picture of a square brick building. The sign over the door says "BANK" but the building is clearly abandoned. Now, if students are not paying attention to the date, they read this photo as a poetic image of the slow depopulation of small town America. Even when I point out the photograph was made during the Great Depression, they still read it as a generic document of hard times. I explain that in the days before saving accounts were guaranteed, a closed bank meant that any money that had been deposited there was simply gone, never to be recovered. Then they finally see the specificity of place, time, and context. The photo was taken at a time when "one-third of a nation" was "ill-housed, ill-clad, ill- nourished," to quote Franklin Roosevelt's second inaugural speech. Rather than receiving it as a generalized image of the Great Depression, the students begin to understand the gravity the photo conveyed.

I have been teaching with this image for years, but now I see it evolving. As we live through the Great Recession, my students see the little brick building as a warning and an analog. The temporal context of the work is changing, and the historical present is re-charging the work. Rothstein's photo is now an image both of past loss, and chill foreboding.

I am drawn to historic sites as an artist, the way Géricault and Leutze were drawn to the heroic stories of their time. Historic sites are palimpsests: places where stories are inscribed and re-inscribed on top of other stories. Some of those stories serve as arguments for why each site should be set aside and preserved. But as a practical matter, these places are often empty—not visited, or if people do visit, they do so only once. As a rule these spaces don't play active roles in shaping contemporary cultural debates or discussions. So these sites, which make claims on our landscape and pocketbooks and through which our public history is told, remain at the margins. They are like hanging curveballs, or ripe figs. They wait for imaginative and creative engagement. They offer opportunities that paintings or

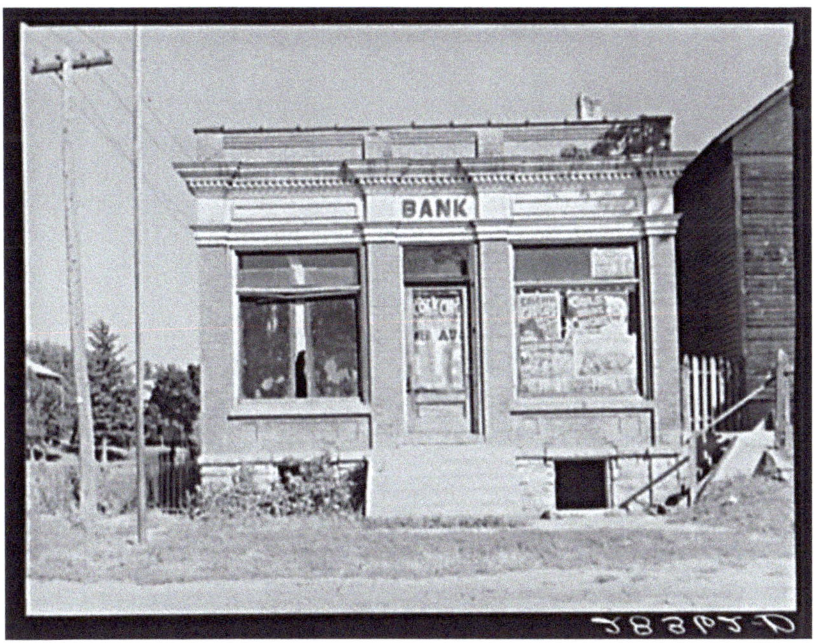

Arthur Rothstein, *Closed Bank. Haverhill Iowa,* 1939
Farm Security Administration/Office of War Information Black-and-White-Negatives

photographs never could: the simultaneity of various histories embodied in a physical space, available at once.

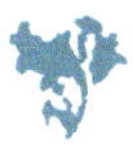

Imagine a mansion built in 1890. The place may be preserved because of the architect or owner. But that is not necessarily the only thing, or even the main thing, that interests contemporary audiences. In such a place, an artist may choose to make work about the servants, and in so doing raise questions about such contemporary issues as labor rights or immigration. The artist may engage the broader narrative of women's history or of the neighborhood that has changed around the house. These questions are about how we understand the relationship of historic "fact" to "cultural truth," and how new meanings might emerge.

A historic site is similar to an object in a museum—it has been removed from the marketplace, assigned a particular kind of cultural value, and protected. These historic sites are grounded in an economic, social, material, and geographic specificity. They are in a different category from other sorts of places and contribute to how we make sense of the past in a particular sort of way. Claims of truth and authenticity are essential to public history—and to the places we preserve as historic sites. They form a shared symbolic matrix that helps define us as citizens. Questions arise: Whose story gets told and who gets to tell it? What has been edited out, censored, or left behind? What insights could an imaginative interaction with the historic record offer us? Artists can examine the way we have been shaped by our official histories as well as by our collective, overlooked stories, or the evocative possibilities that spin out from them—unearthing forgotten narratives and posing alternative readings.

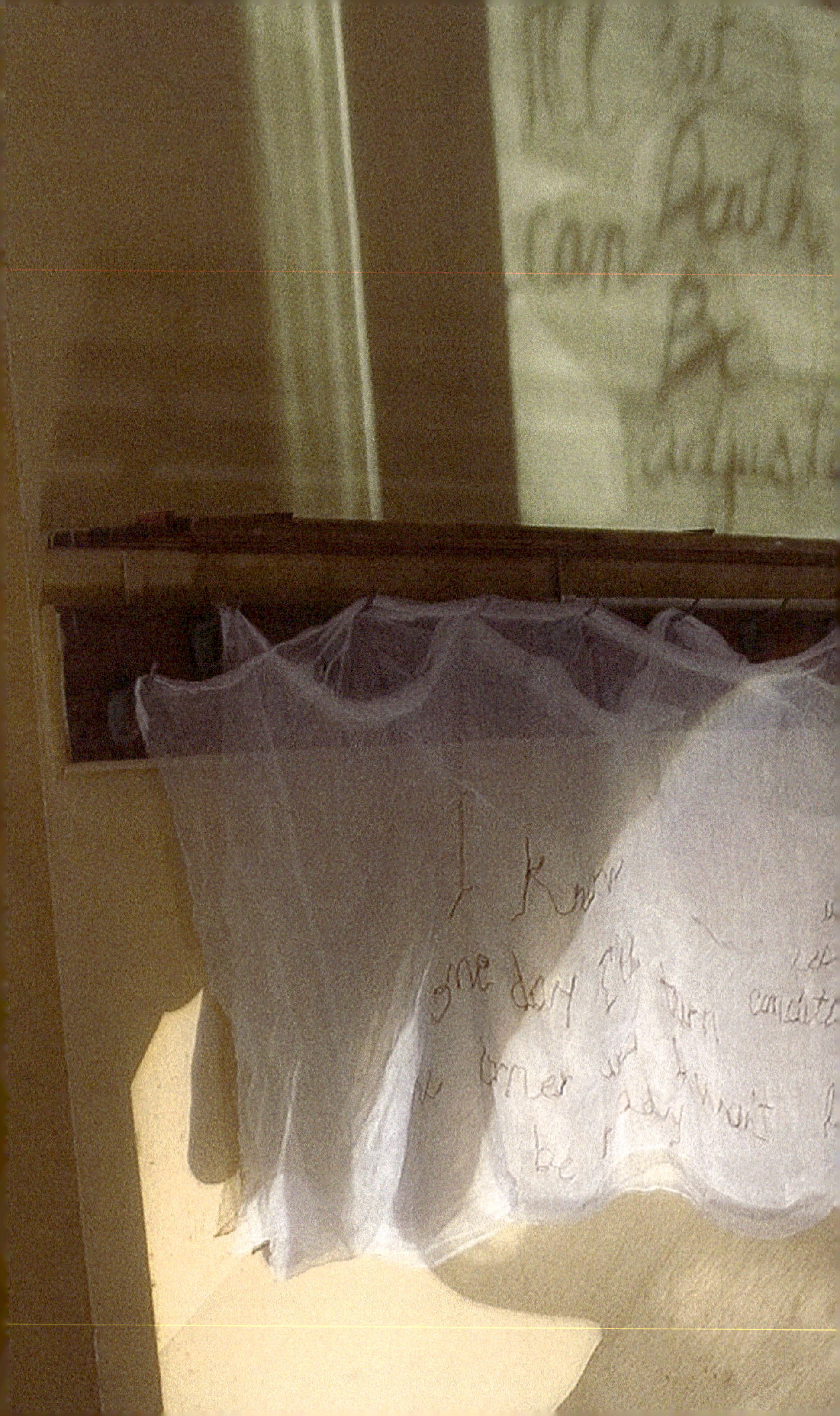

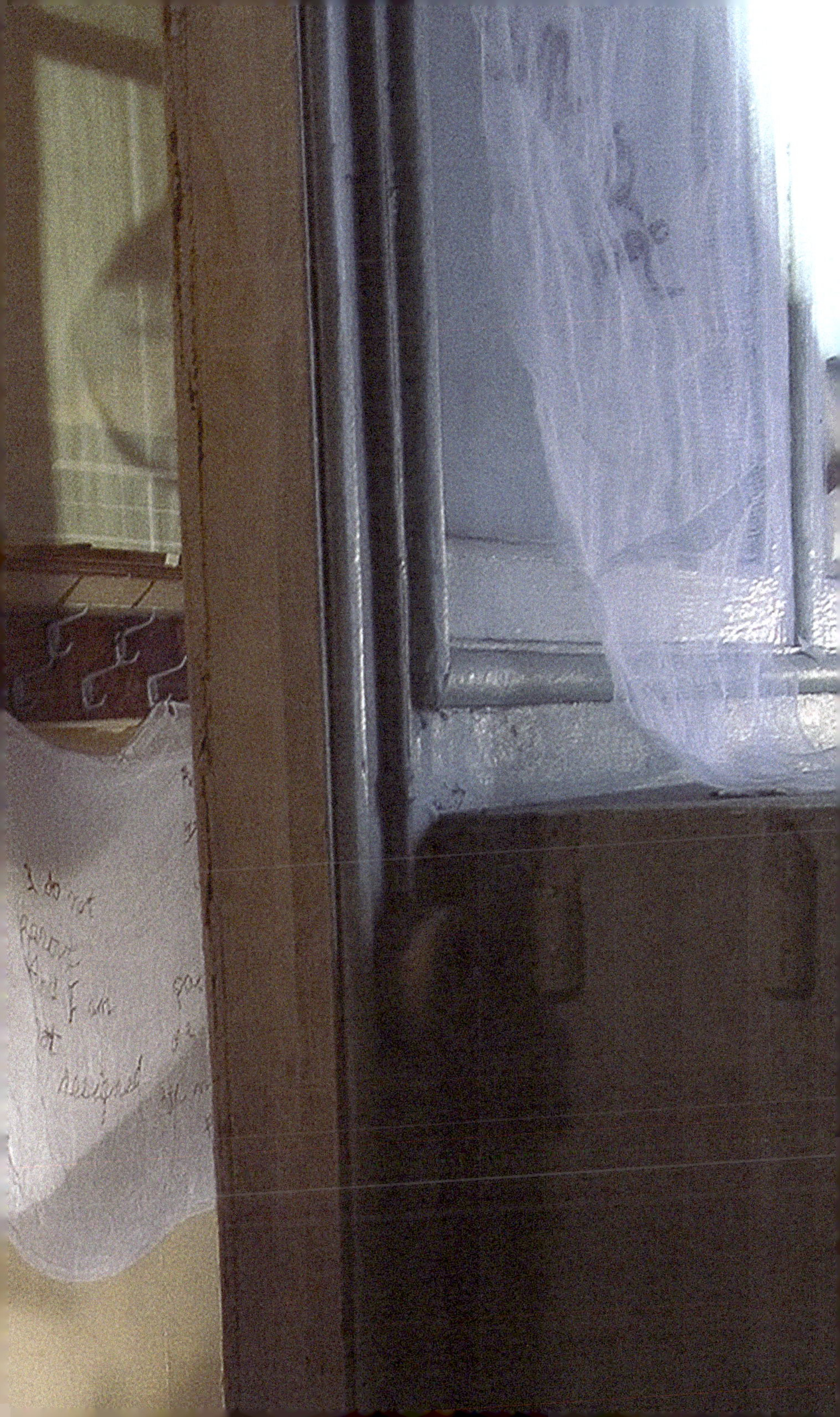

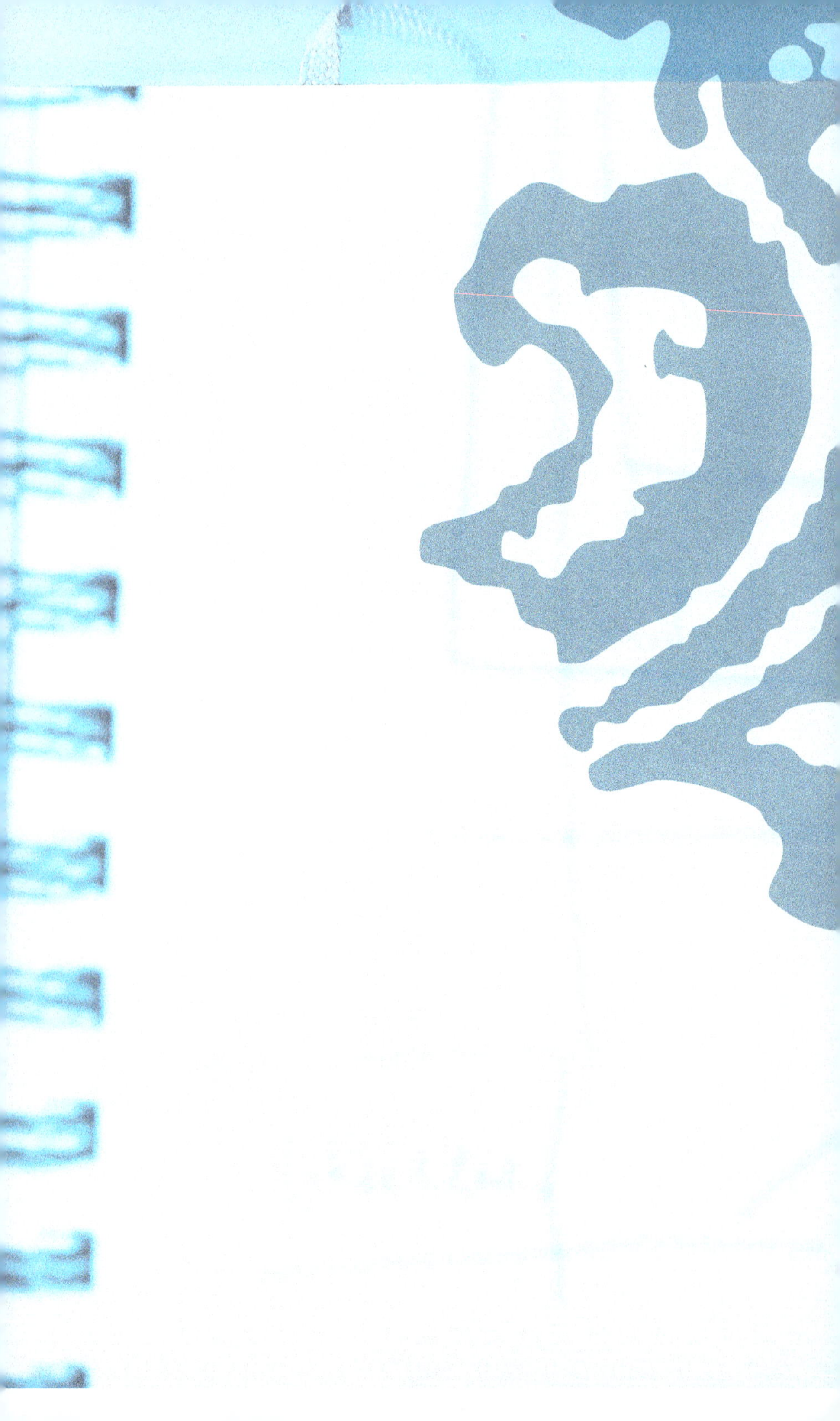

about excavating history

rebecca keller

beginnings

The past is never dead. It's not even past.
William Faulkner

The quote from Faulkner nagged at my brain as I walked through the Glessner House Museum, where I was invited to do an exhibition. I had been creating politically inflected and socially engaged work, often site-generated, for several years, and the curator wanted me to create something for the newly renovated "white box" gallery adjacent to the main historic house. But the more I thought about it, the more a different sort of project stirred in my imagination. What was taking shape in

previous spread: Rebecca Keller, *All But Death Can Be Adjusted*, 2006

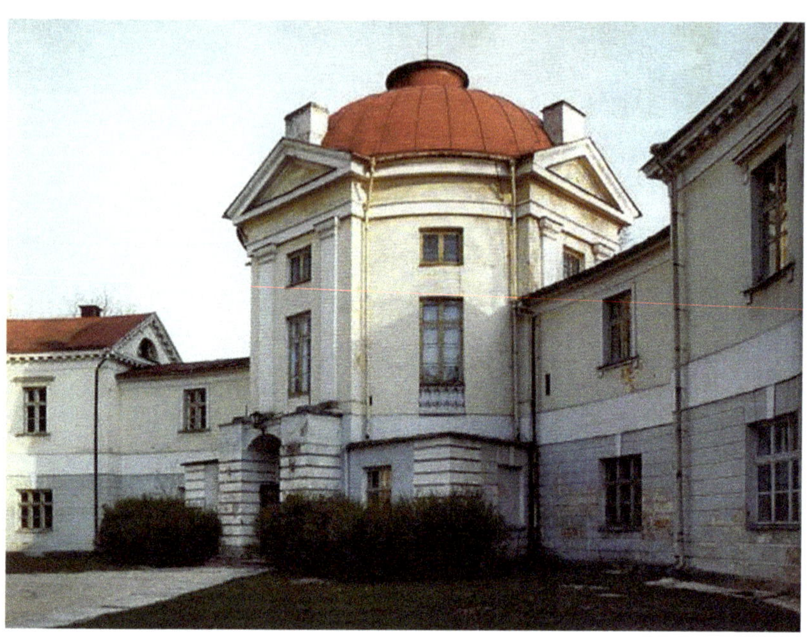

exterior of the 1801 Anatomy Theater building, Tartu, Estonia

my brain departed from a traditional exhibition of objects, and also differed from the practice of artists reinstalling museum collections. Though I didn't know it yet, the resulting exhibition would draw on my background as an artist: my work teaching about the connections between art, institutions, and the body politic; my interest in the narrative domain of history; and my increasingly research-driven art practice.

Fast-forward a few months. I was heading to Tartu, Estonia, where I had earlier been a Fulbright professor, to work with graduate students and to install an exhibition.

In Estonia, I arrived to find that due to unanticipated complications, my earlier plans had to be scrapped. Serendipity struck as I was talking with my colleague Ana in her office. Her phone rang, and she switched to Estonian, a language I had been spectacularly unsuccessful in learning. However, with her occasional slips into English, the contextual clues, and a few half-remembered verbs, I derived an inkling of what the conversation was about: finding space for graduate student studios during the upcoming summer months. The person on the other end of the phone was telling her that these students would be allowed to use part of an old anatomical theater, circa 1801.

The anatomy theater was a half-empty building at the top of a shady hill. The city had vague plans to renovate, but beyond the few rooms that housed an "exhibition" on medicine—a haphazard grouping of old photos and things moldering in jars—the building was unused. Without quite knowing why, or what I would do, I heard myself blurt out, "Let me use it!" when Ana hung up.

She looked at me as if I had sprouted horns, but I got more excited the more I thought about it. Let me use it, I repeated.

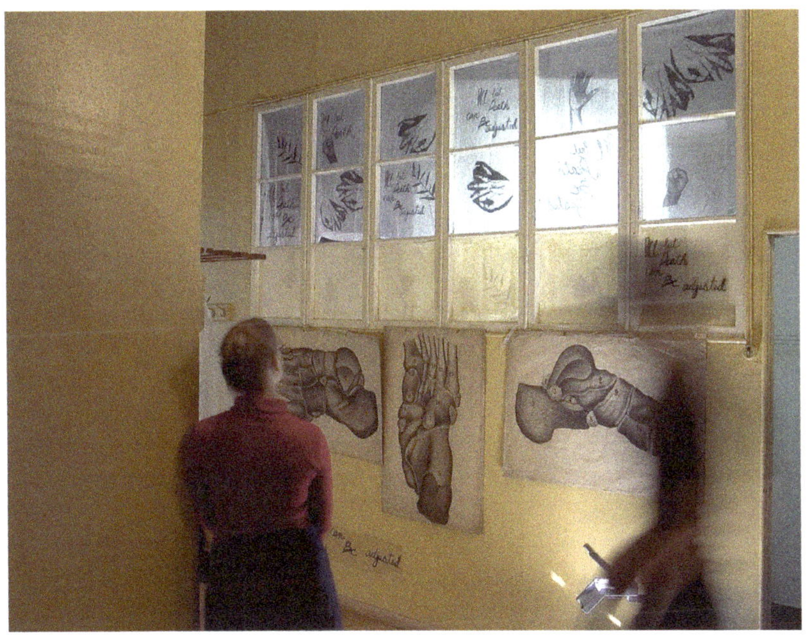

Rebecca Keller
All But Death Can Be Adjusted, 2006
bandage gauze, embroidery, projection, text, ink, 6 x 20 feet
1801 Anatomy Theater, Tartu Estonia

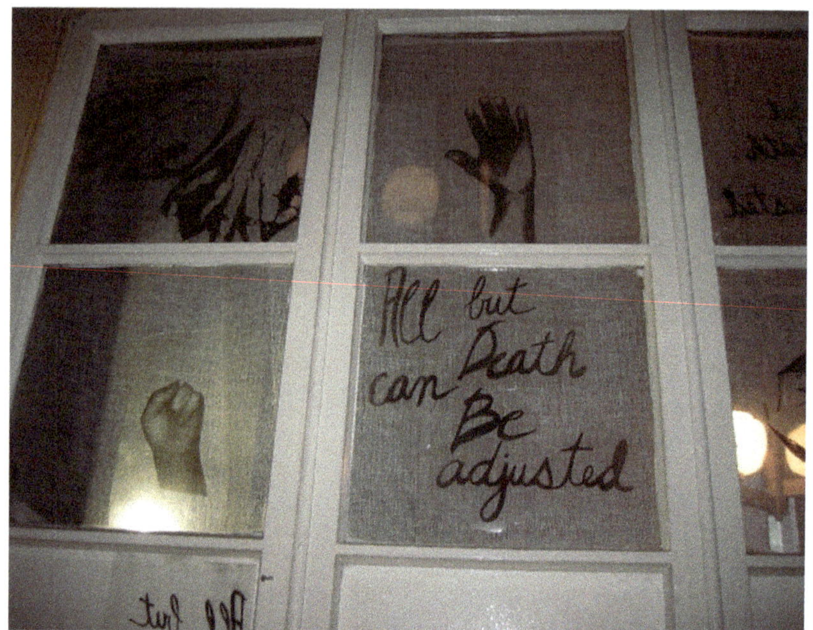

All but Death Can Be Adjusted (detail). These windows were made of special glass to focus light into the interior of the building (built before electricity), which made them ideal as projectors.

I'll do a project with some grad students—a crash course in site-generated and site-responsive work.

Ana was skeptical. But she redialed. I could tell by her tone that the idea was not met with enthusiasm; as soon as there was interest in making and situating art in the space, suddenly the people in charge saw it as a place that had to be regulated and protected. The day before, no one would have known or cared about a piece of cracked linoleum or a 1950s paint job. But now, because I wanted to work there, suddenly every surface was too precious or fragile to touch. (This is a phenomenon that grew familiar as I went farther into this sort of work.)

How Ana got the approval, whether she actually did go through channels, or in the end simply decided that there was no one other than herself that needed to approve it, I don't know.

following spread: Rebecca Keller, *All But Death Can Be Adjusted*, 2006

Sometimes it is better not to ask.[1] But what was clear was that I had only three weeks. Period. As often happens, limitations spark creativity.

I began to research the site and to brainstorm materials that were portable, appropriate, and suggestive. I embroidered bandage gauze with quotes from poets and scientists and draped it where lab coats once hung; I used the series of internal windows that originally transmitted light to the interior of the structure (built before electricity) to create a series of projections. I sutured the peeling organic cork that lined the floor, activating the crumbling building as a metaphor for an aging body. Finally, responding to a coincidence that seemed too good to be true, I linked the theater—(where the dead were "anatomized") to the building next door—the maternity hospital—by lining the walk with the type of candle used in Orthodox baptisms and funerals.

I remember that exhibition—*Artistic Operations/Anatomy Theater*—with satisfaction, and also with pride in my students who rose to the challenges of site specificity, extreme time constraints, collaborative demands, and limitations on what could be touched, altered, etc. But in addition to the satisfaction there was a certain level of frustration. If only there had been more time, and more materials in English. The constraints made some works we had conceived impossible to accomplish.[2]

---

1. Sometimes it is unclear just who exactly has the authority to say yes to something like this. And in that vacuum, the easiest, safest answer is generally no.

2. Logistics in these projects can be extremely difficult, and the project in Estonia—because of language as well as issues with transport and access—was particularly hairy. However, limitations can work in one's favor: the site was so evocative that having a short time frame helped winnow out some ideas that were great but not practicable. Sometimes I wish these sites would be available two or three times, so several iterations of these ideas could be explored.

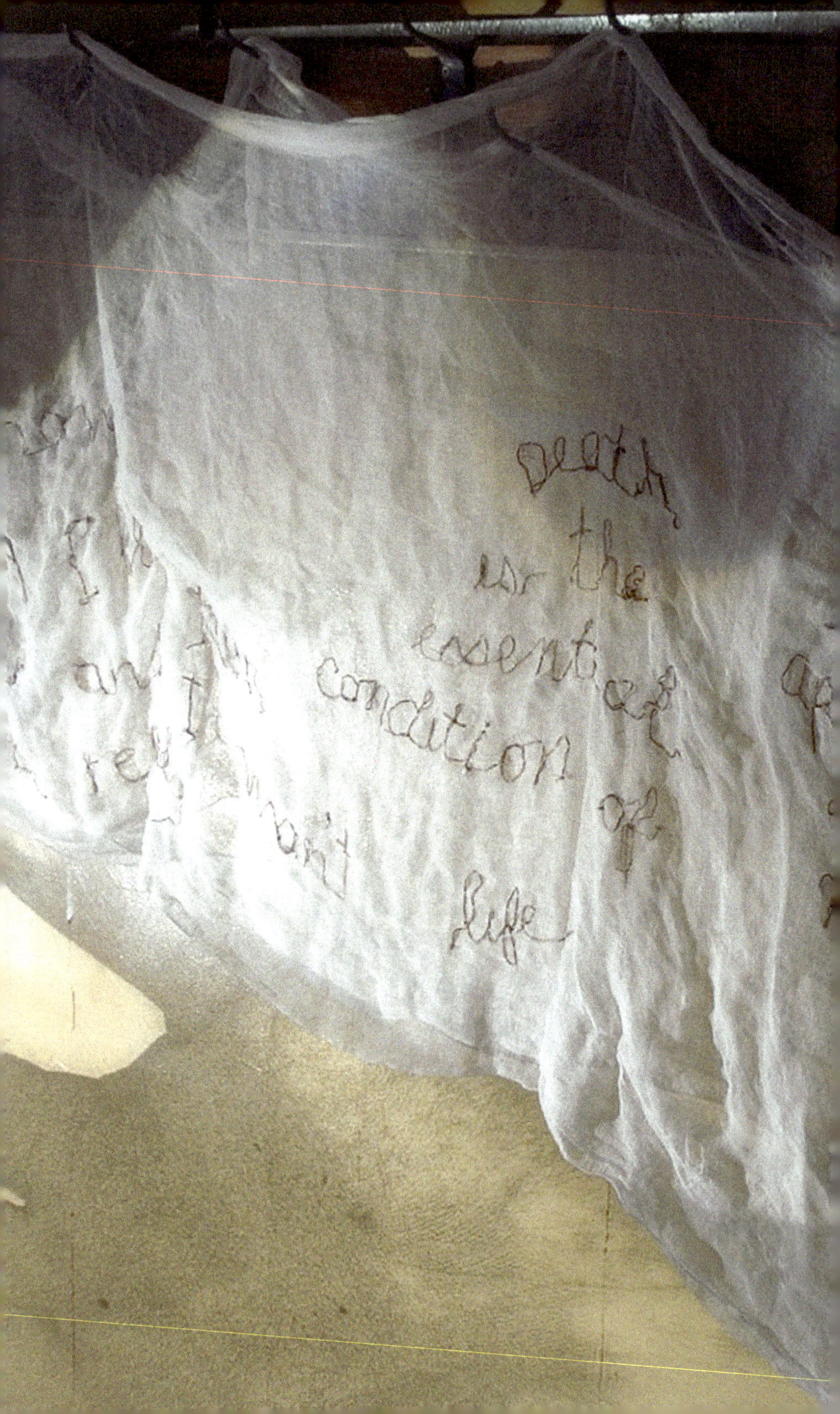

Death
is the
essential
condition
of
life

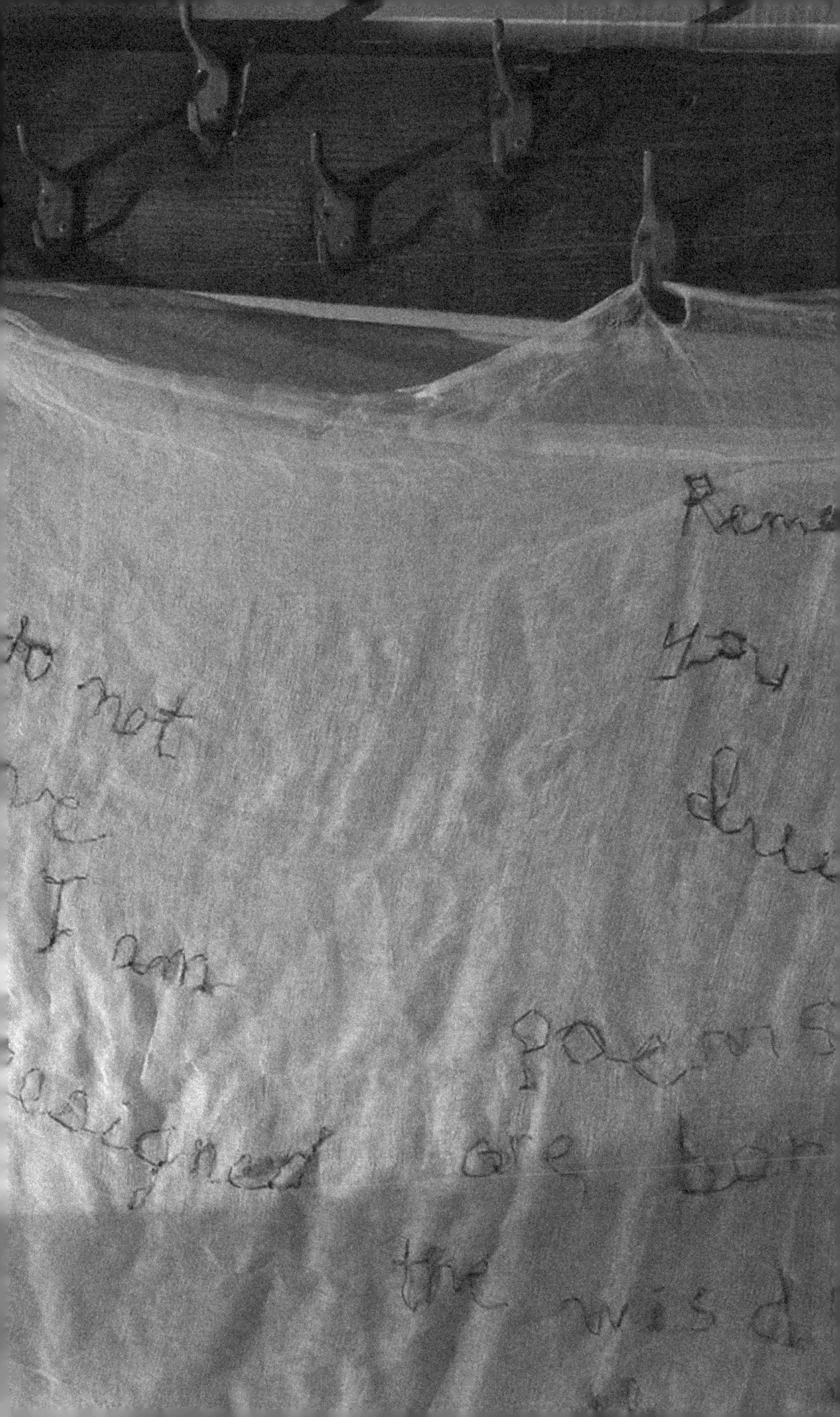
you
I am
are
the

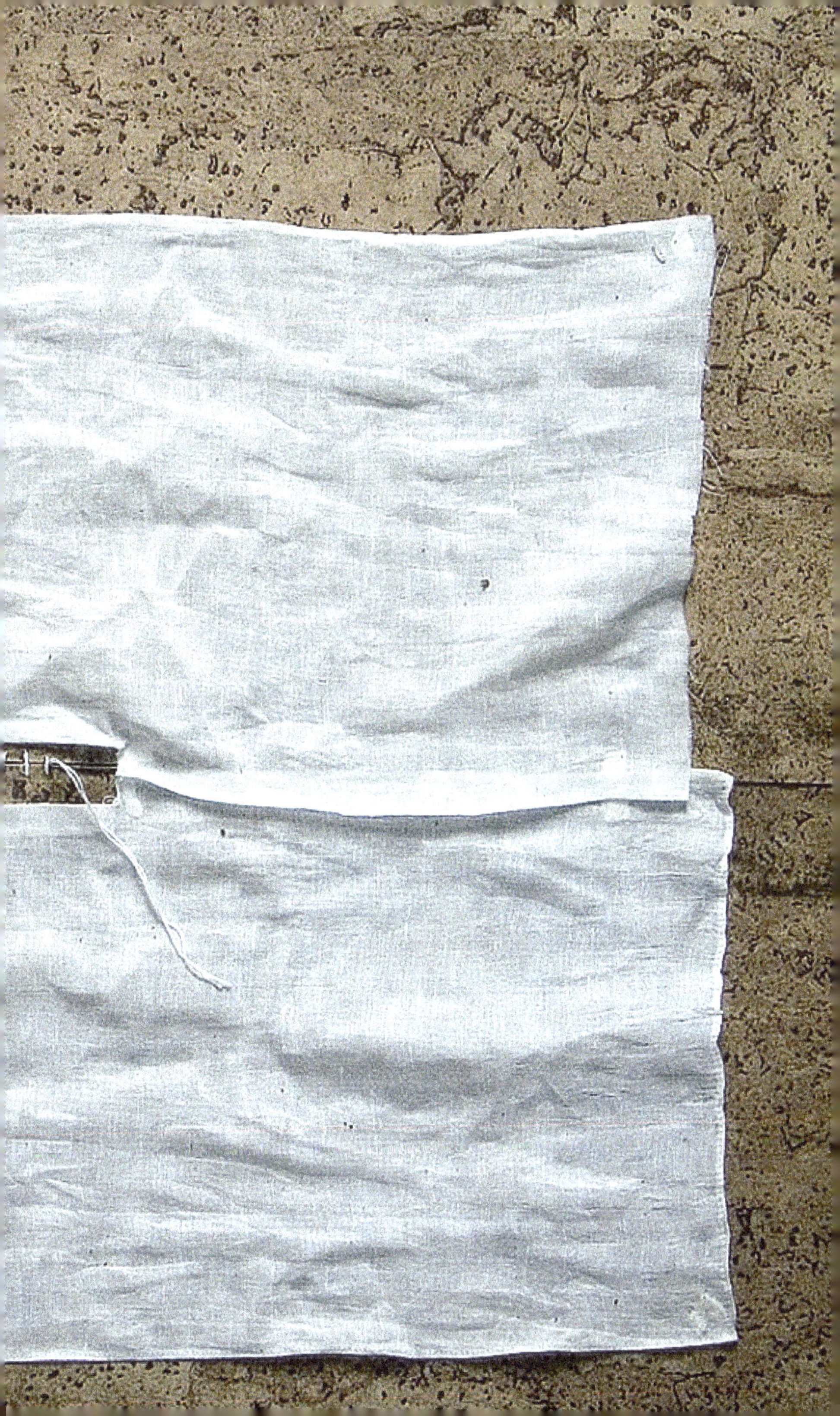

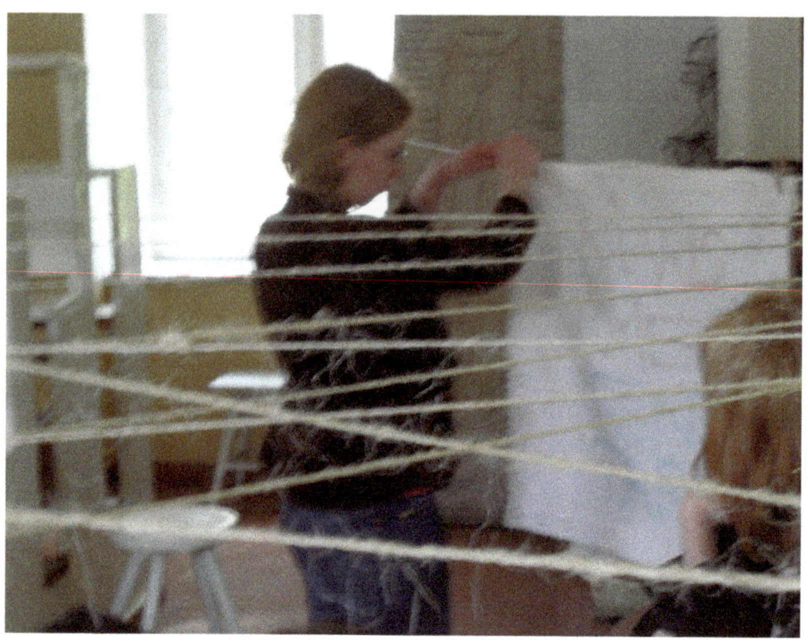

Participatory performance/intervention in the Anatomy Theater, Tartu, Estonia

When I returned to Chicago, I delved into research on the Glessner house, plowing through information from the U.S. Bureau of Labor Statistics, Census Data, numerous sources ranging from history to journalism to letters, and other original documents.

The usual reason given for the importance of the Glessner house is that it is one of the few private residences designed by H.H. Richardson. But there is more to the story. The Glessners worked closely with Richardson as he designed it, and the resulting building was less an example of a particular style than a reflection of the way the Glessners lived. It gave architectural form to the social fabric of the day.

For example, the Glessners asked Richardson to design the home so that the servants could go about their work without having to pass though family areas. In response, Richardson built a house with a series of service hallways that made this

previous spread: Rebecca Keller, *Floor Suture*, 2006
original 1801 cork floor, 'repaired' with surgical suture, and linen drape

possible. In another example, the architectural design even related to gender roles: since men had other job options, having a butler was a status symbol, and homeowners would want the butler to be seen. Accordingly, in the Glessner house, the butler's pantry is a border zone, mediating the space between the servant areas and the family rooms so that the butler alone was visible to guests. Likewise the schoolroom is situated halfway between the entrance and the main floor: the tutor, though not exactly a servant, was certainly not of equal status with the family.

I wanted to comment on the social and economic relationships the house made manifest. The resulting exhibition, *Home/Work, House/Work: A Meditation on Labor*, focused on the house as a workplace, and told stories of class, immigration, and gender. The exhibition flowed from the conviction that meanings buried

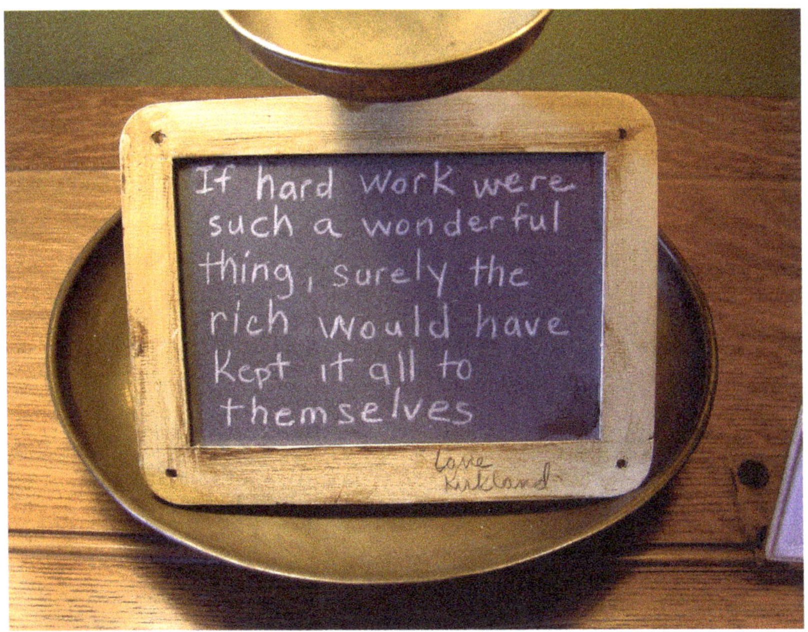

Rebecca Keller, *"Surely the rich would keep it...",* 2006
vintage slateboard, chalk, 5 x 7 inches
From *Home/Work, House/Work: a Meditation on Labor* at the Glessner House Museum, vintage slate with quote from a labor leader, in the classroom. Pieces in this room examined how education sometimes reinforces class expectations.

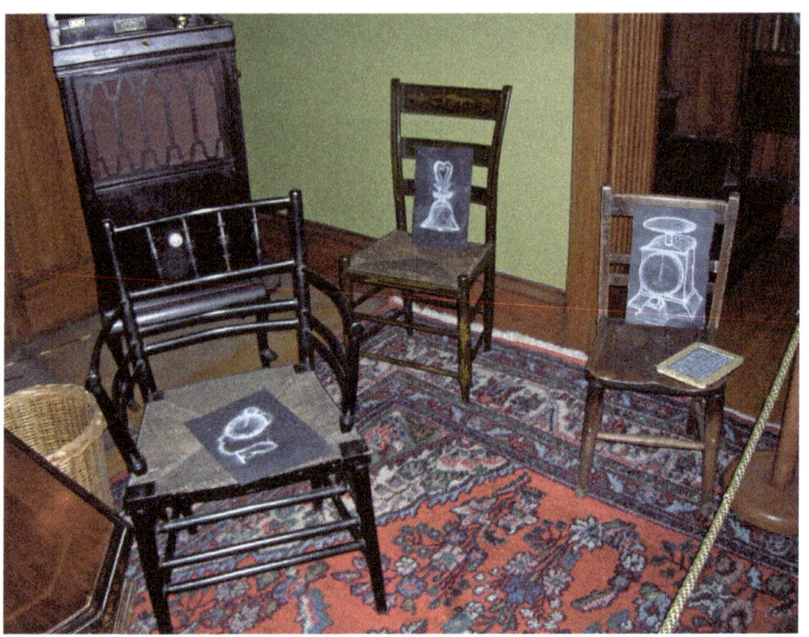

Rebecca Keller, *Take Your Place...*, 2006
vintage slates, chalk, three drawings, each 12 x 10 inches
From *Home/Work House/Work: a Meditation on Labor.* Vintage slate with images that evoked types of work and methods of control.

in the house could be connected to contemporary social and community issues.

Making the artwork meant identifying materials and processes most appropriate to the task at hand. I did drawings on curtains, sewed Victorian-style servant's aprons, and transformed the bell jars in the pantry into bar graphs. I used repainted and altered vintage burlap sacks, silver trays, vintage photos, and lead type. The objects and interventions were integrated into the house so the whole was more than the sum of its parts.

It is important to note that pursuing this project meant securing the deep cooperation of the museum. While I needed access to the space and valuable collections, I also wanted the freedom to shift the focus away from Richardson and the house and toward social issues that were both uncomfortable in general and could be taken as implicitly critical of the Glessners in particular.[3]

Fortunately the Glessner staff were passionate about their subject, and interested in ideas and history. As people committed to the success of the museum, they welcomed the opportunity to broaden the interpretive framework of the house, and saw the exhibition as a way to offer repeat visitors a new experience. It could also draw new visitors: the audience for contemporary art and historic sites didn't necessarily always overlap. This project offered the museum the chance to participate in the culture in a more dynamic way.

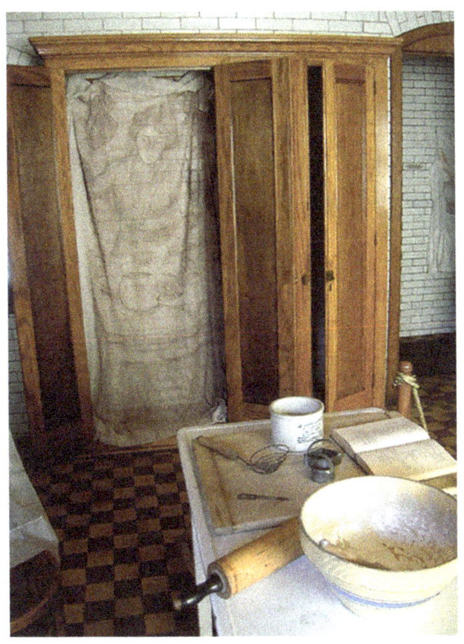

Rebecca Keller, *Unseen in Plain Sight...*, 2006
sepia drawing on vintage curtain, 10 x 5 feet
From *Home/Work House/Work: a Meditation on Labor.*
The images used throughout the house were based on archival photos.

following pages: Rebecca Keller, *Dining Room/Workroom*, 2006, Aprons and other working clothing were key motifs in the exhibition. Here the dining room is cordoned off by stained work shirts, and the chair is draped with a drawing of hands gripping a broom. A quote from a housemaid is displayed in the fireplace.

---

3. No one exists outside of economic or social systems: not the Glessners, and not us. As the research into domestic labor at the Glessner House progressed I saw echoes in contemporary life: domestic work, if hired out, is still largely done by immigrants, is still gendered, and is still poorly paid. We still want it to be invisible. I was determined that the exhibition not be an exercise in finger pointing or superiority, but an examination and, as the title implied, a meditation, on labor, specifically housework.

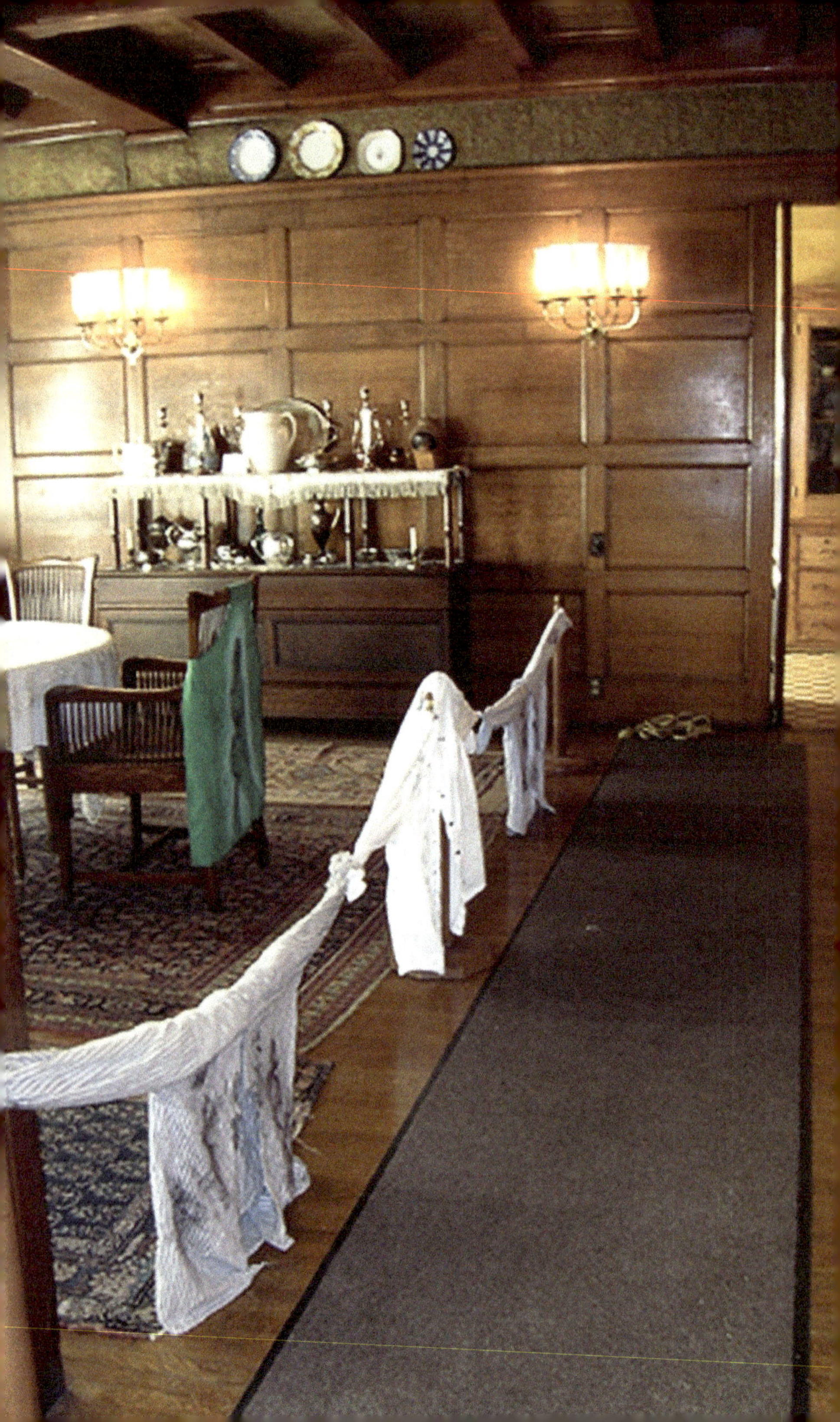

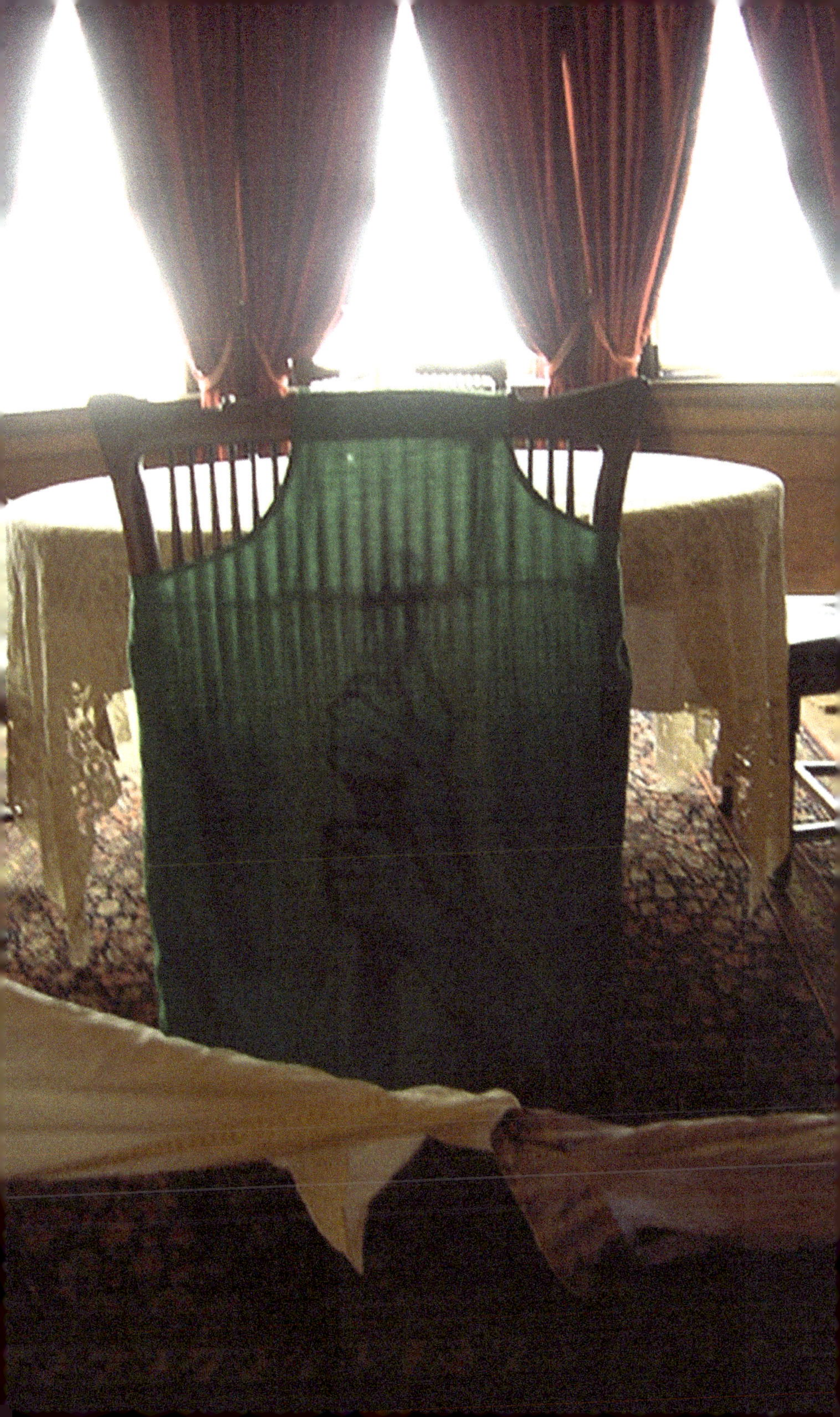

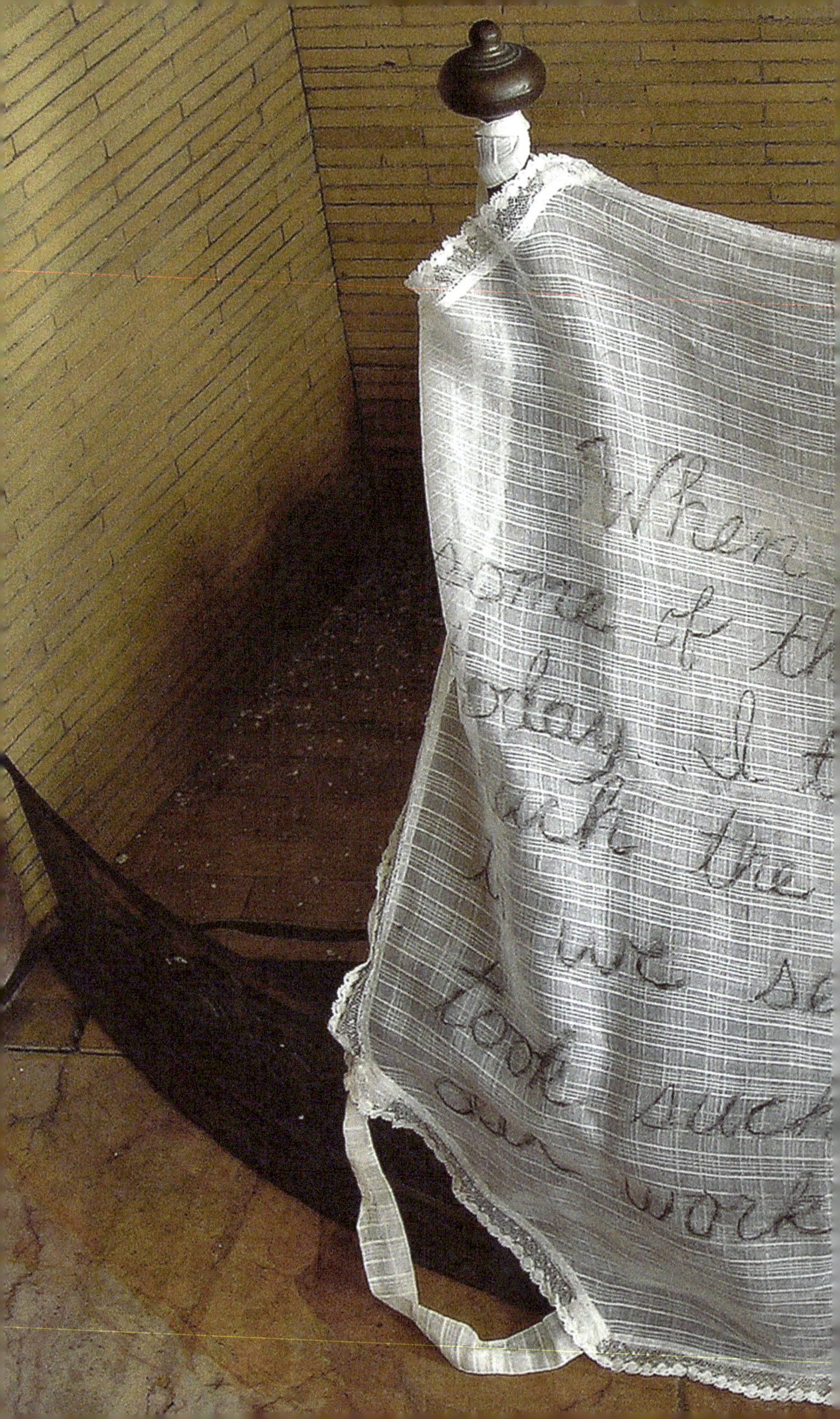
When
some of th
today I t
ask the
we s
took such
our work

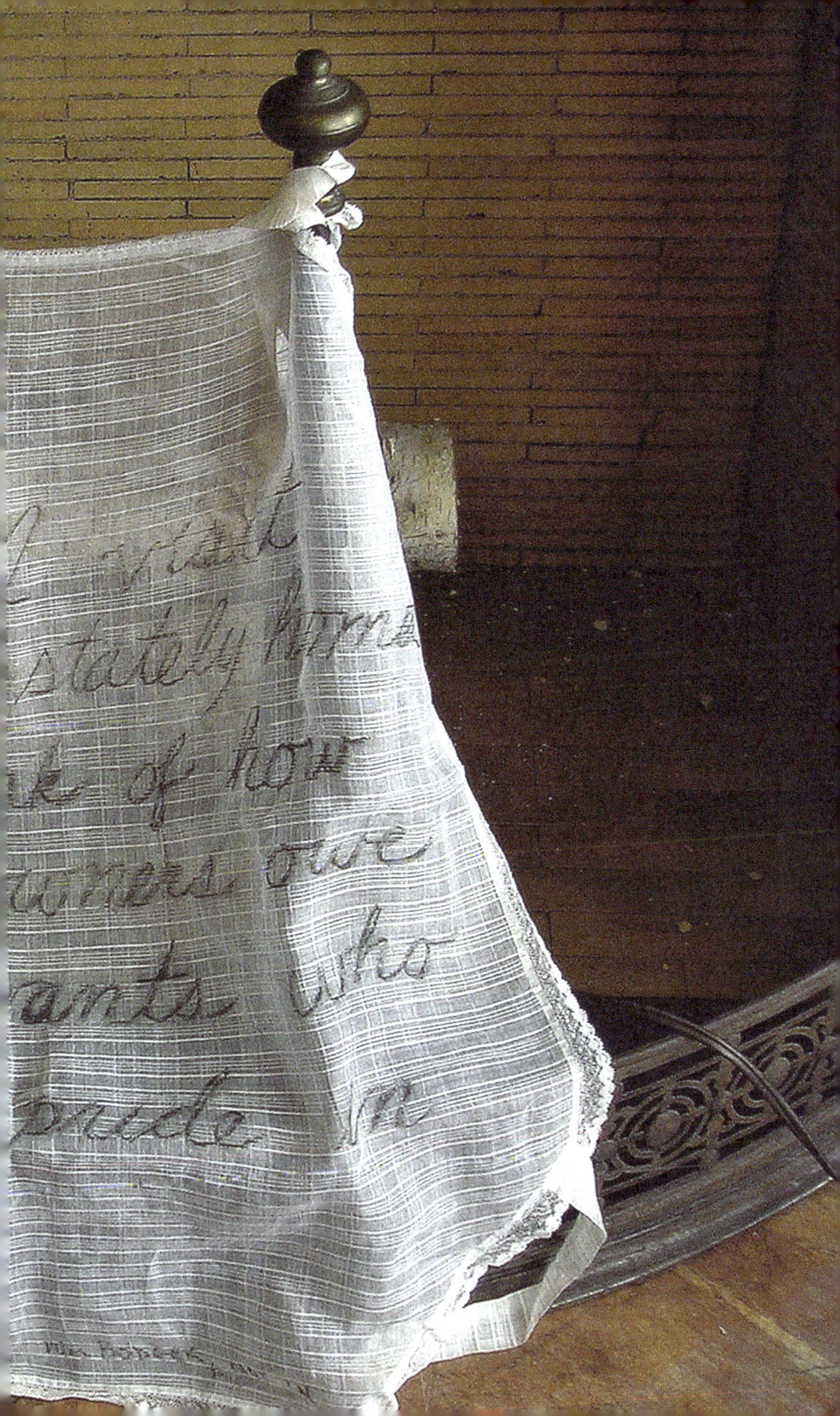
visit
stately hom
k of how
owners owe
ants who

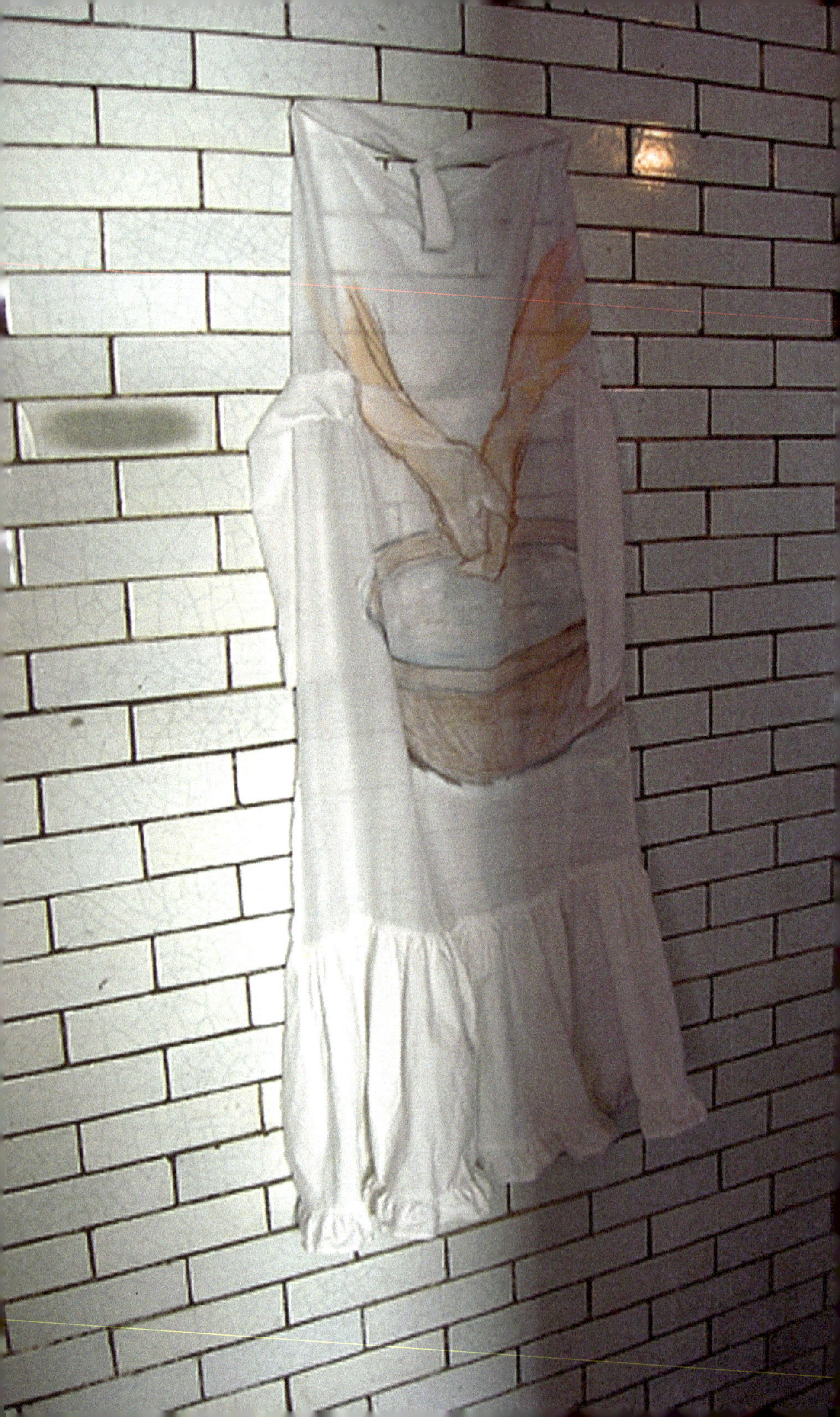

evolution / iterations

For me, a specific site is generative: it is not incidental. In these projects, the artwork is both *site-generated* (based on considerable research into the particular qualities, histories, and contexts the site presents) *and site-responsive* (made in creative response to the research as well as to the physical and social aspects of the site). Perhaps it is more accurate to say that the artists become part of the signifying work the site is already presenting—the art contributes to a place that is actively generating meaning. When we argue with or amplify or complicate that voice, we become complicit in that communication: hence the phrase *site- complicit* artwork.

Sol LeWitt famously said, "The idea becomes a machine that makes the art." In these projects the *site becomes a conceptual and material engine that drives the work,* both in its physical manifestation as well as in terms of content and audience.

My work continues to evolve. In 2011, I was invited by SubCity Projects to do a project in the former studio of Lorado Taft. Taft was an enormously important artist in his time—he was even referred to as the "Dean of American Sculpture," a reputation he solidified when he published a popular book on the subject. He was also a successful teacher. The picture of Taft that emerges is one of a knowledgeable, ambitious artist with almost evangelical vision. These traits are brought into vivid focus in a scheme he embarked on near the end of his life: creating a "Dream Museum."

The idea was simple but grandiose: A huge building would perch, temple-like, on a hill overlooking Los Angeles. The interior, consisting of an enormous room (750 feet long, with 80 foot ceilings) would house a collection of ancient sculptures from all over the world, arranged by culture and era. The grid, organized with regions/cultures along one dimension, and chronologically along the other, would, in Taft's words, "reveal the meaning of life."

How did Taft imagine he'd acquire these works of art? Easy: he wouldn't. The original sculptures would be represented by exact life sized plaster reproductions. In this, Taft exposes a fascinating throwback to a once heated battle among museums in this country, known as the "battle of the casts"; it was waged during the early years of the 20th century between the people who thought that casts of the great sculptures of Greece and Rome should be in museums for the educational and aesthetic benefit of the public, and those who felt that it was only in the original work that the spirit and *soul* of the art could communicate itself to the connoisseur.

While doing research into Taft, I came across a compelling image. Taft didn't only imagine his enormous museum in California; he also had developed a traveling version—a sort of kit—for use by teachers. The kit held miniature reproductions of sculptures from the ancient world along with small pedestals and directions for use. I found a brochure advertising the kit with an image of the model sculptures set up in Taft's preferred arrangement.

This brochure, along with the architecture of the Fine Arts Building (where SubCity Projects and Taft's former studio are located) furnished my conceptual and design cues. SubCity Projects uses a tiny space with an old-fashioned wooden door with a window. I realized it was a perfect set-up for a diorama. I treated the space as a vitrine to hold artifacts that mimicked the Dream Museum: in effect, making a model of a model. In the rear of the space I hung a huge architectural sketch, based on notes and actual renderings Taft left for the building he envisioned. In front of the drawing are tall, narrow pedestals, each holding a handmade model of one of the ancient statues that Taft had hoped to include in his museum. It felt as if I were unpacking a set of Russian dolls, each one referencing the one that encased it.

Taft's Dream Museum reverberates in particular ways through contemporary artistic concerns: Appropriation. Public pedagogy. Cultural literacy and authority. The idea of masterpieces. The notion that artists have a stake in others learning about art. That art should be in elementary and high schools. For me, it

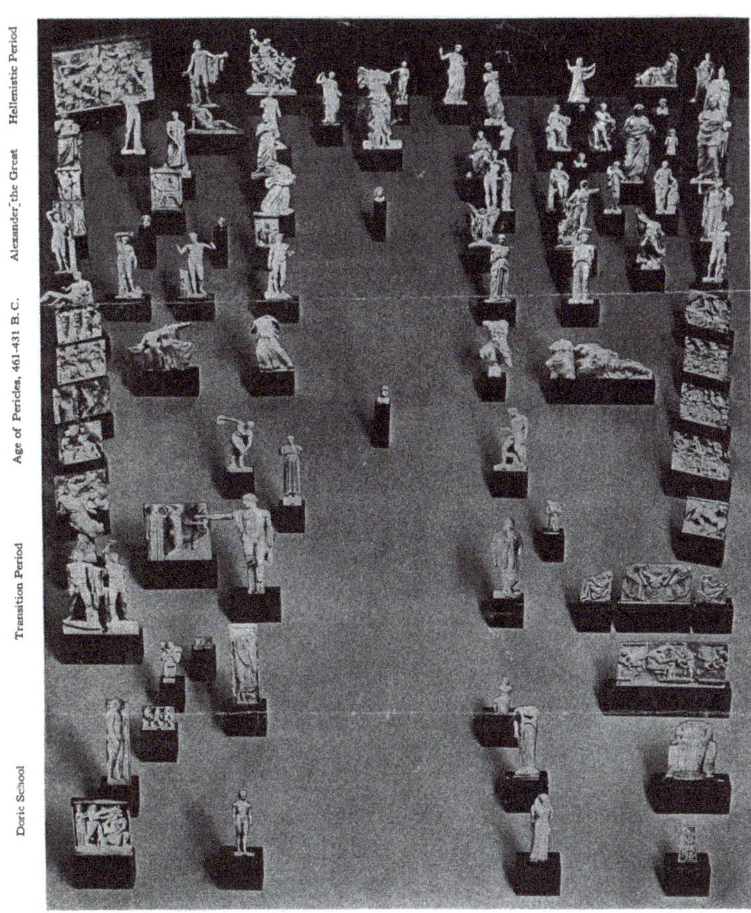

Here is Lorado Taft's Little Museum just as it will look when mounted on plywood and fitted to pedestals (complete instructions included with each set). Arrangement shown is Mr. Taft's favorite. Through using the set you will discover dozens of other possible arrangements.

Here is a practical art appreciation project developed by a master teacher and a famous sculptor ready for use in your school.

was a prime example of site-based research leading to surprising connections with many aspects of my work as a teacher, museum person, and artist.

truth, value, and pedagogy

Despite these examples, it continues to be challenging to convince the directors of historic sites, and especially of historic houses, to permit artists to work with these physically fragile and culturally protected sites. Usually people assume

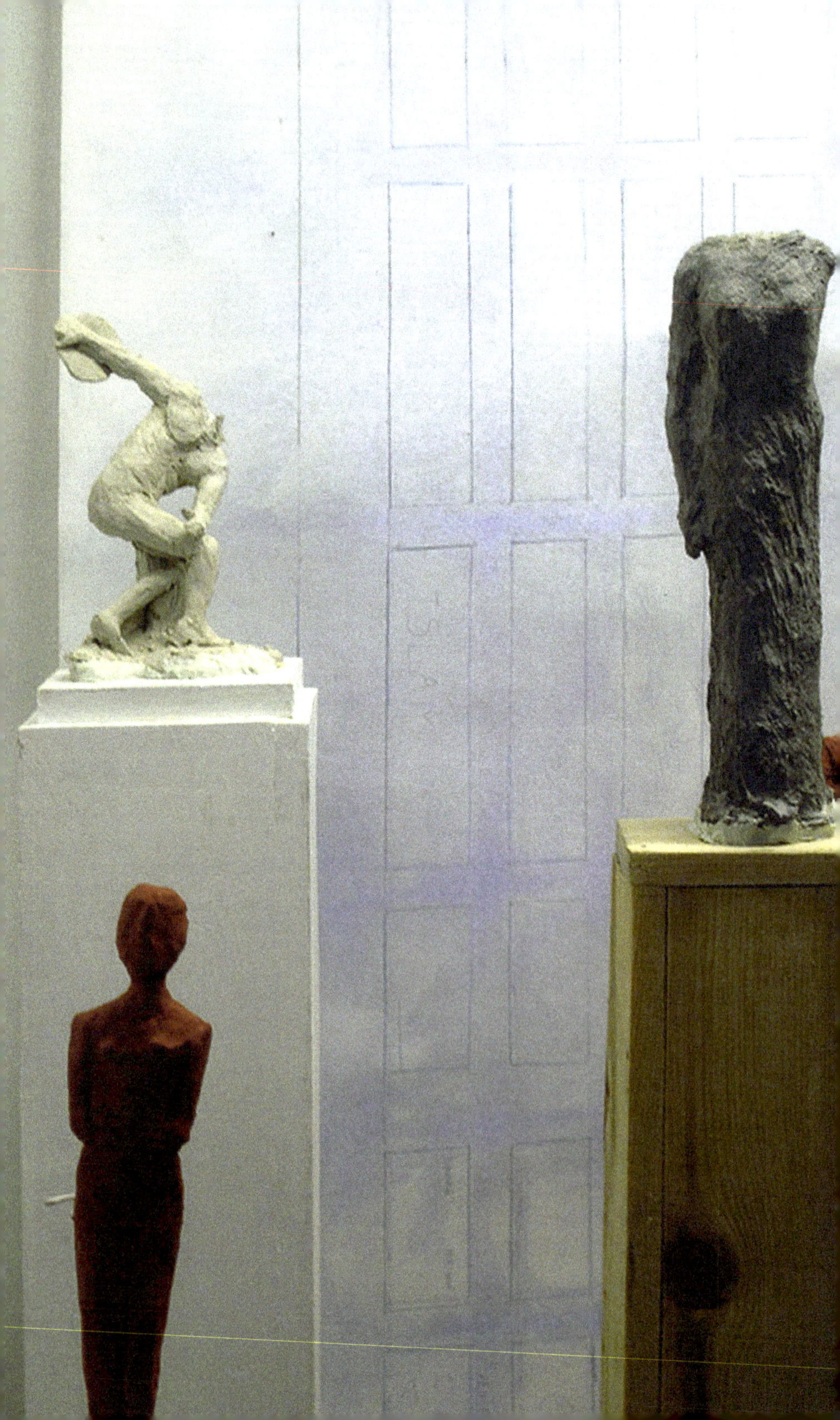

the possible conflicts are about exposing less-than-savory facts about a heroic person, or uncovering stories that don't square with the master narrative. But most museums are aware that a single master narrative does not serve them well and actively try to present a variety of points of view. The larger and perhaps more interesting question has to do with truth-value.

Truth claims are important to museums. They are important to the discipline of history, and to our understanding of place. They are especially important, in fact almost essential, for public historic sites. But an artist may want to run with a story, taking it beyond what can be documented and proven. The artist might want to imagine the servant in the room, the child of the famous man, the immigrant worker cleaning the balustrade. We might move into speculative and imaginative areas—ideas suggested by the research but not provable. In fact, the imagination is a prime way that people interact with historic sites. But complicating an agreed-upon narrative with speculative or fictive material can pose a difficult situation for the staff of a museum. Though such speculative artworks may open up the site in new and exciting ways, they may also require the institution to stretch in uncomfortable directions.

These projects have helped me to develop a methodology and process that continues to evolve. They also made me think about the sheer number of historic sites and the types of claims they make (or more often, fail to make) on our collective imaginations. I realized that these exhibitions were a type of public pedagogy, a way of speaking our collective history through multiple voices. I was aware from my other classes how gratifying students found making connections with historical and social material. And given the many ideas that spin out of the research, I was aware that many voices working in collaboration could result in richer narratives.[4]

---

4. A collaborative approach to research is particularly fruitful. In the development stage, before anyone has started making anything or even has a clear idea what they will do, the sharing of research and the different ways the same piece of information can be seen and received makes the eventual work richer. Because the

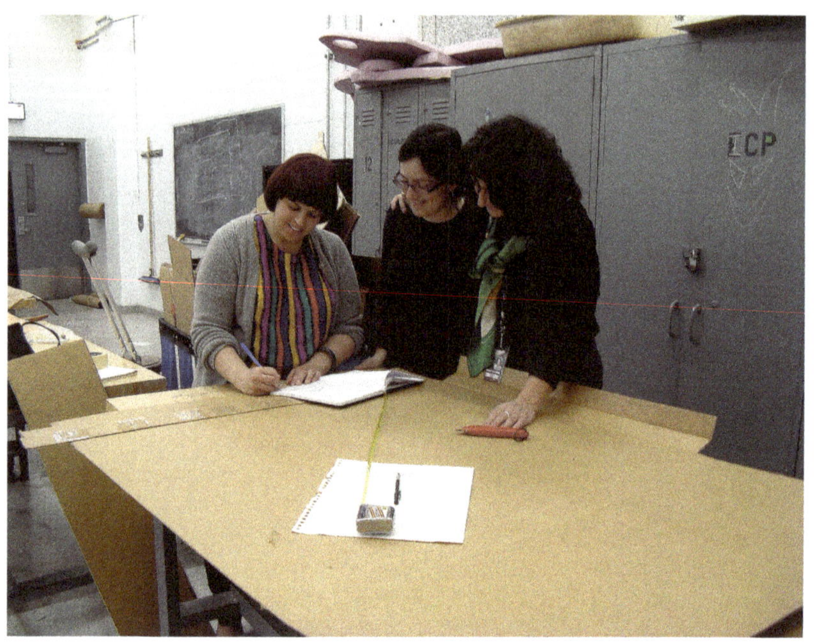

page 48: Rebecca Keller, 2011, Lorado Taft's Dream Museum, SubCity Projects
above: Working in the studio at the School of the Art Insitutte of Chicago. (Rebecca Hernandez, Liene Bosquê, Rebecca Keller)
following pages: In the studio (Chiara Galimberti, Rebecca Keller)

In 2008, Mary Jane Jacob, an important and innovative curator, was chair of the sculpture department at the School of the Art Institute of Chicago where I teach. Jacob had seen and liked the Glessner exhibition. I approached her with an idea:

---

process is open-ended—including the possibility that discussions might NOT end in a formal collaborative work—the ideas and projects take shape organically, in response to the environment and stimulus of the ideas around them, each growing where another one casts light or shade or finds the most nurturing soil. Often a particular event or aspect of the research grabs a number of people, but they all have different takes on it. In the end they might all do separate pieces, but their mutual fascination with the material enriches each artist and also makes for a deeply satisfying exhibition-making process.

if I could find a site that would agree, would she support the creation of a class with an unusual structure—part collaborative/workshop, part research, part exhibition-driven, part exploratory process?

She was very supportive, agreeing to help shepherd the proposal through the SAIC's approval procedure. Meanwhile, I approached Vince Michael, another professor at the school. Vince, too, had seen the Glessner exhibition and had written about it. He is on the board of the National Trust for Historic Sites, and is interested in making these places as dynamic and relevant as possible. Vince pointed me in the direction of several sites he thought might be open to the idea. One of those was the Farson-Mills house, otherwise known as the Pleasant Home. I contacted Laura Thompson, the executive director of the Pleasant Home Foundation, and talked with her about what I had in mind.

It required Laura to take a big gamble. Since what I was planning on doing would involve work from students, I couldn't guarantee what it would look like, what media would be used, even what themes would be engaged. I was asking her to allow us to be partially in residence at "her" historic home; to allow us to impose upon the resources of the collections and the patience of her staff; to occupy the site, intervene in the interpretive scheme, and create an exhibition/intervention in the house. To her huge credit, she agreed.

Excavating History, as a class and collaborative, was off and running.

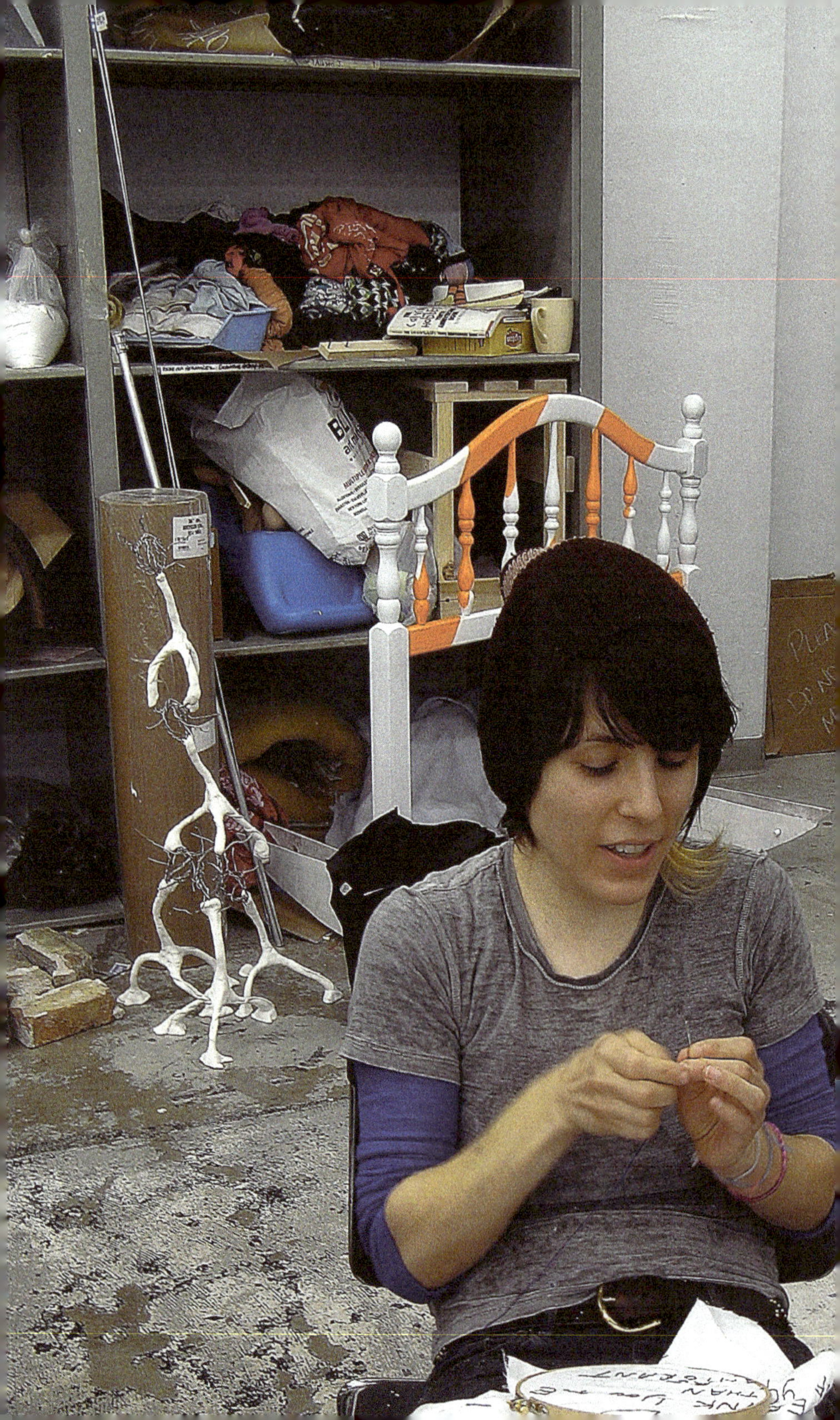

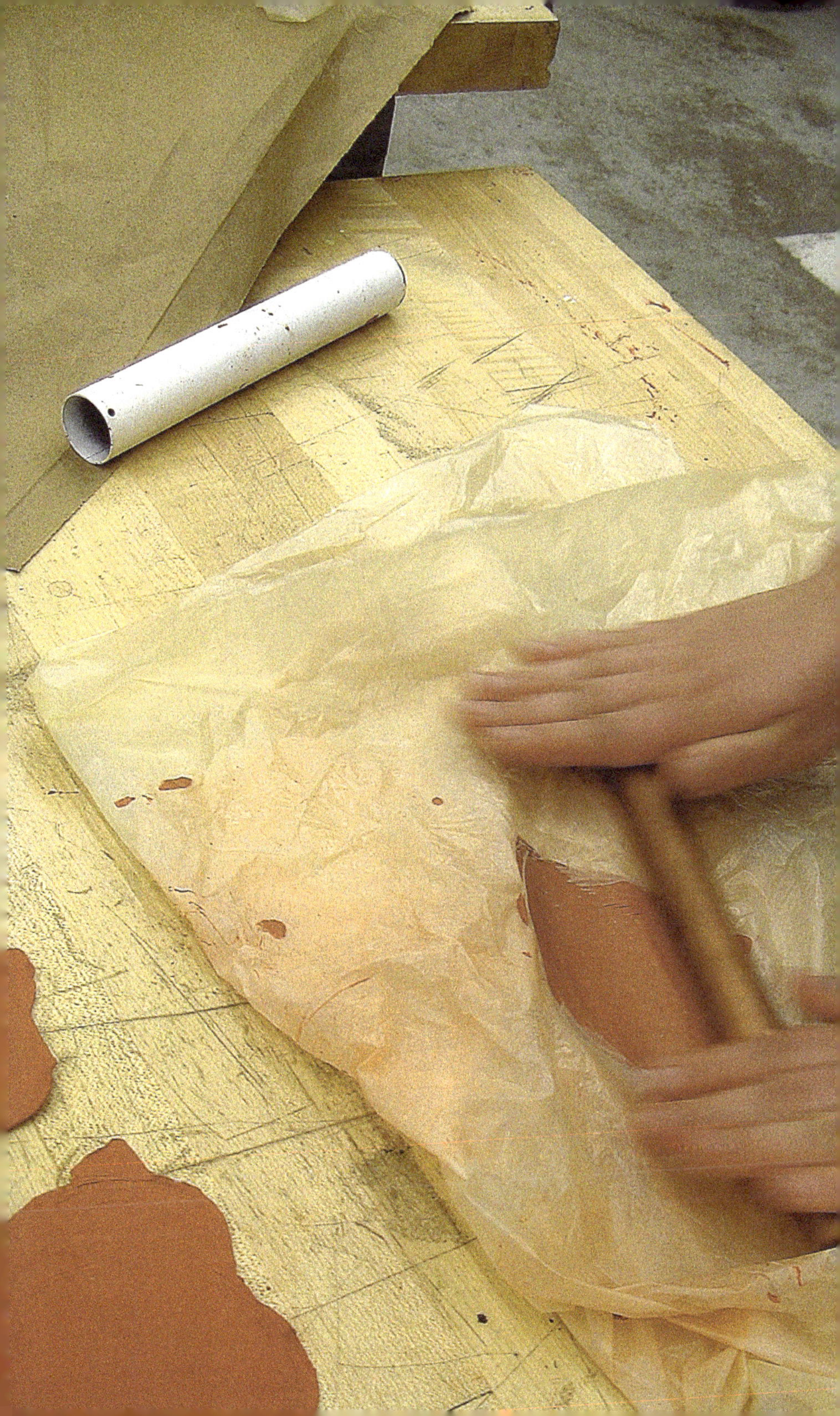

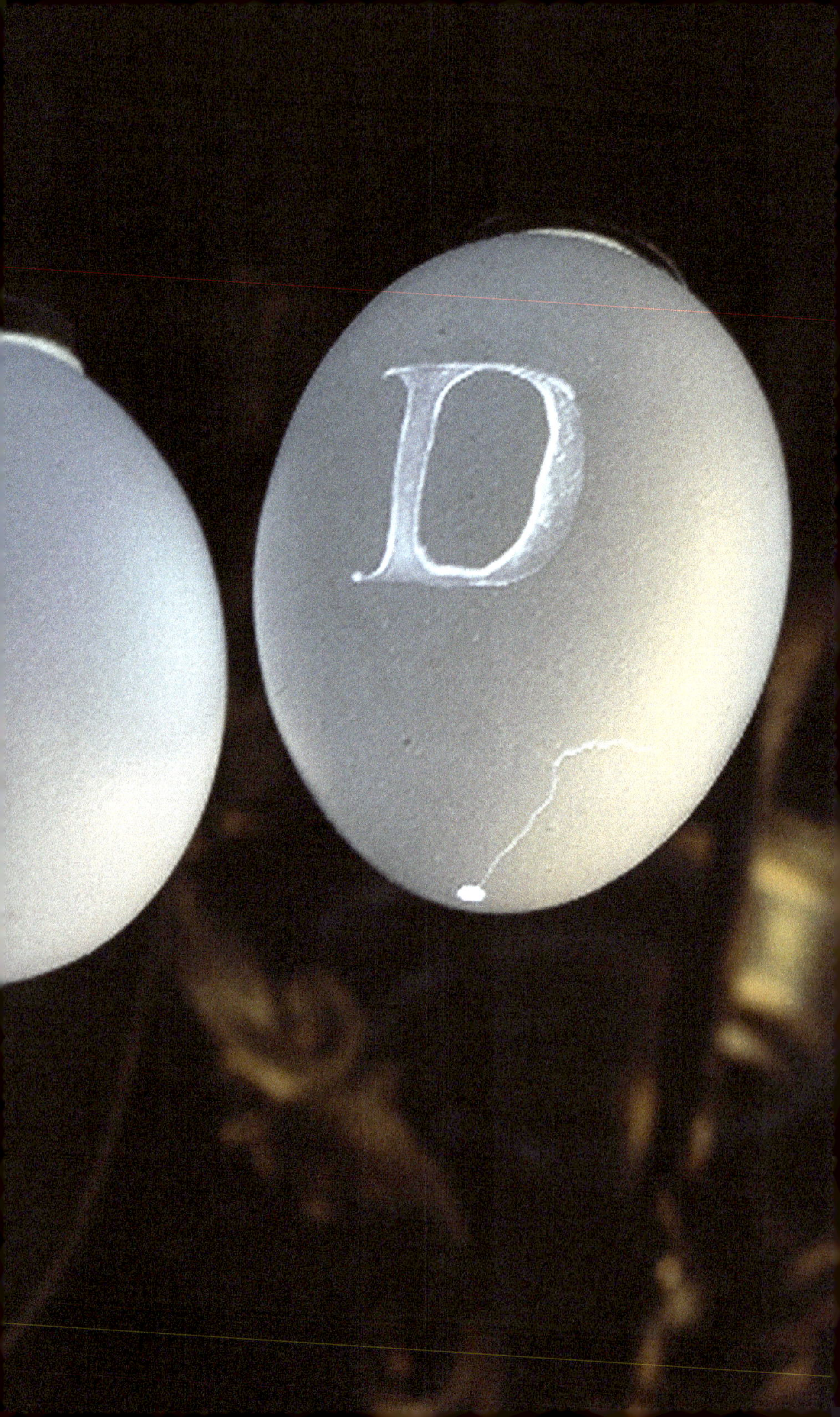
D

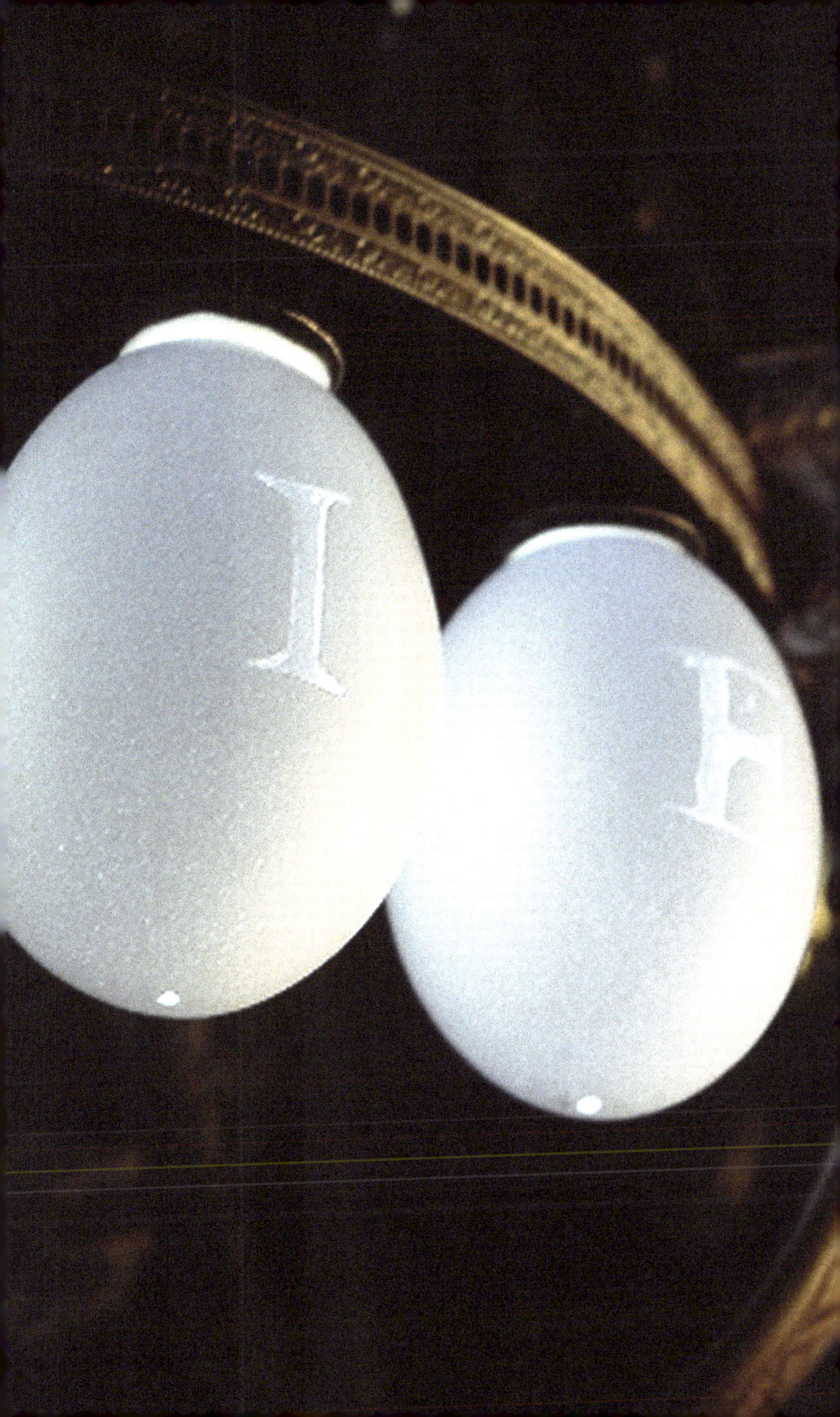

excavating: three years, three sites

History may be described in terms of large sweeping events, but it is also local, peculiar, and personal. The projects described in this book were conceived as a way of exploring what gets left out of the category we call History, especially in its public dimension. They ask which stories get told in our public historic sites and explore how these stories are shaped by cherished myths, political and social agendas, and folklore. Through these projects, visitors are presented with new and poetic ways of reading history, and experience an expanded critical and social dialogue through the inclusion of other voices into the interpretation of our shared past. The artists became researchers and narrators, storytellers and makers. The historic sites are made places for imagination as well as fact.

previous spread: Briana Schweizer, *Last Words*, 2008

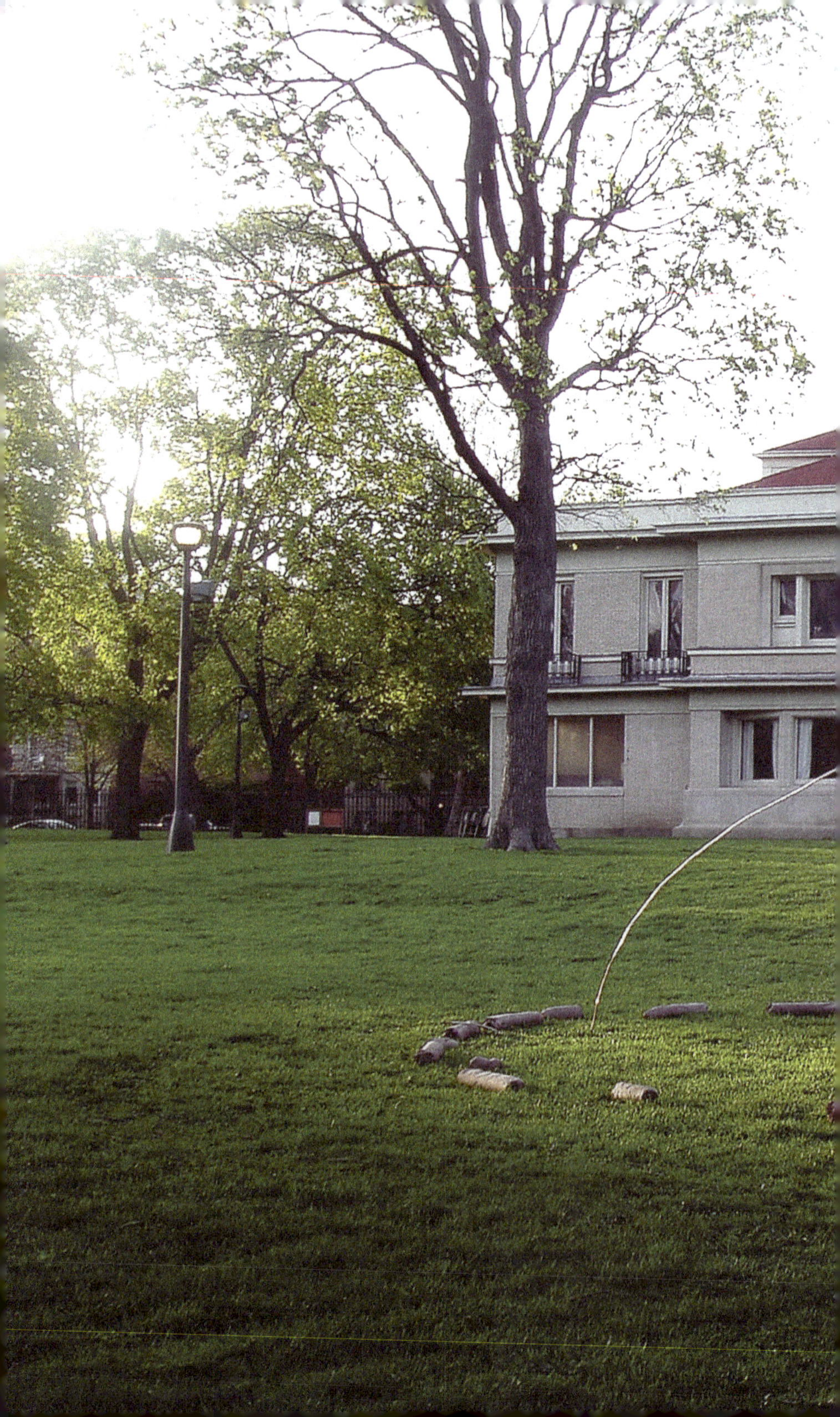

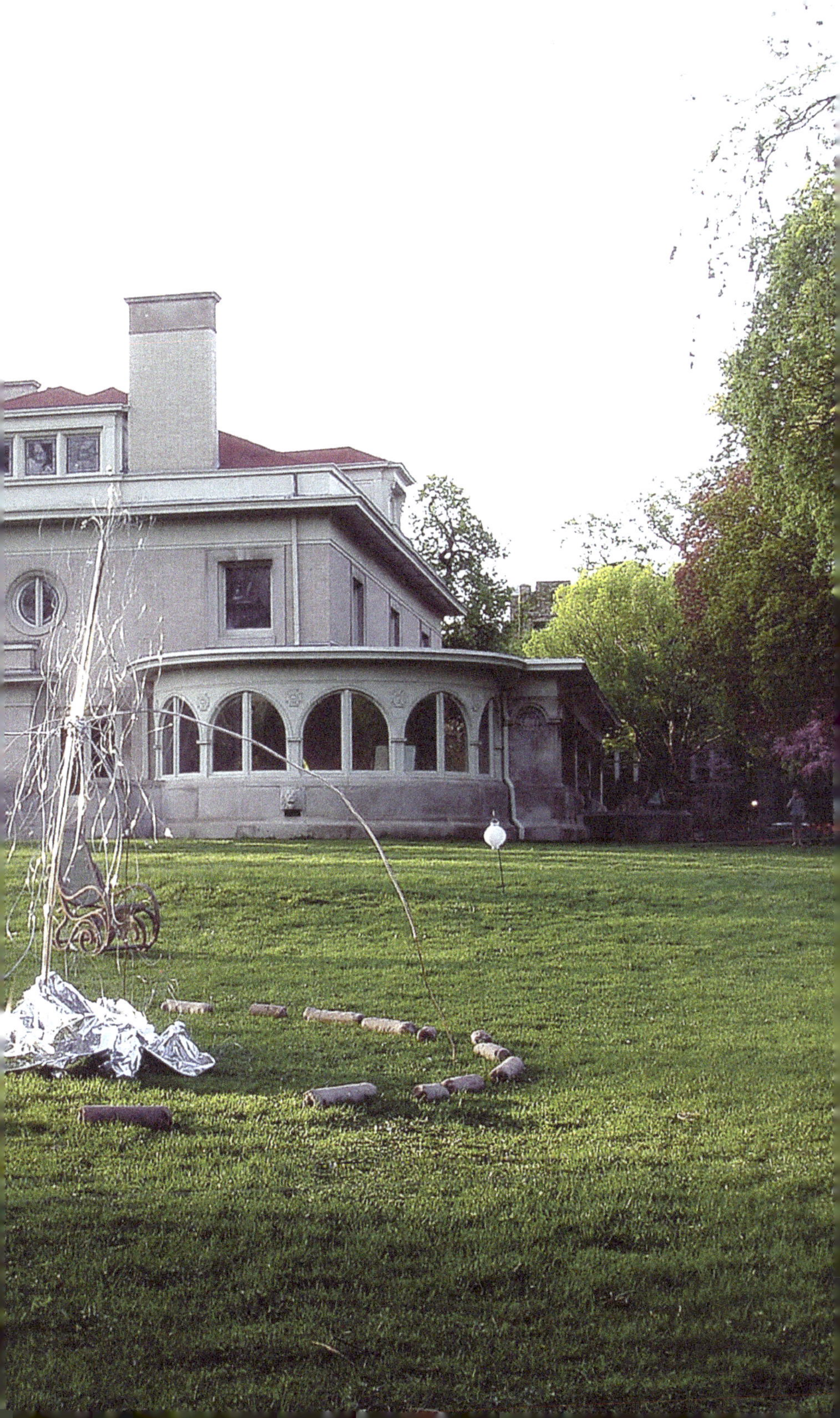

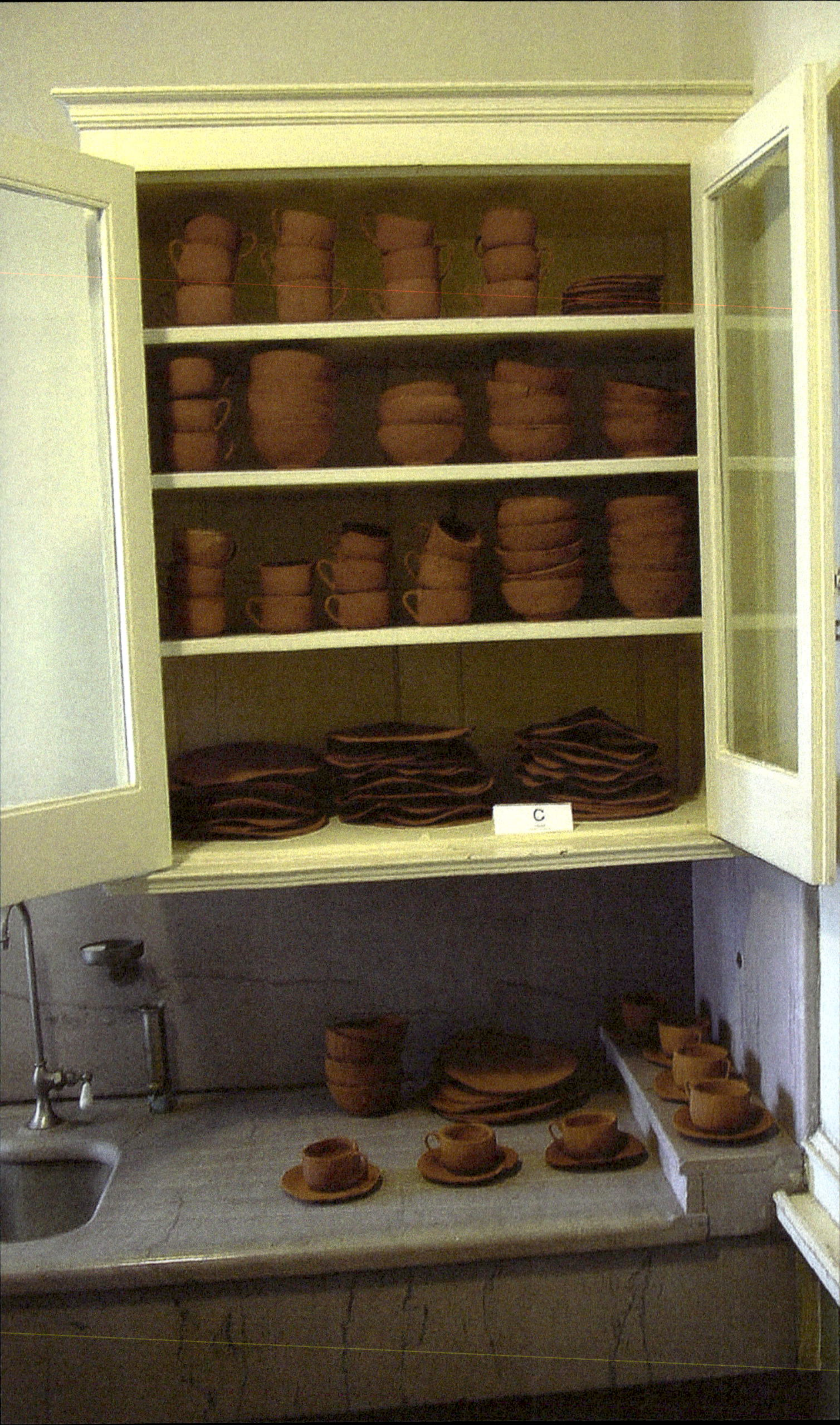
C

excavating the pleasant home 2008

rebecca keller

The Pleasant Home/Farson Mills House was designed by George Maher. (It is situated at the corner of Pleasant Avenue and Home Street. Really.) The 16,000 square foot house is clad in narrow roman brick, with deep porches and eaves, rich interior decoration, including intricate woodwork, stained glass, and repeated decorative motifs, notably a stylized honeysuckle. It sits on a seven-acre park. Today the first floor is interpreted as an architecturally significant house, open to the public. On the upper floors are the offices of the Pleasant Home Foundation and the offices and archives of the Historical Society of Oak Park, as well as the historical society's small exhibition room.

previous spread: June Licata, *Fountain*, 2008, copper, brass, clay, mylar, rocking chair
left: Amber Ginsburg, *C is for Colonize*, 2008, cinnamon, applesauce

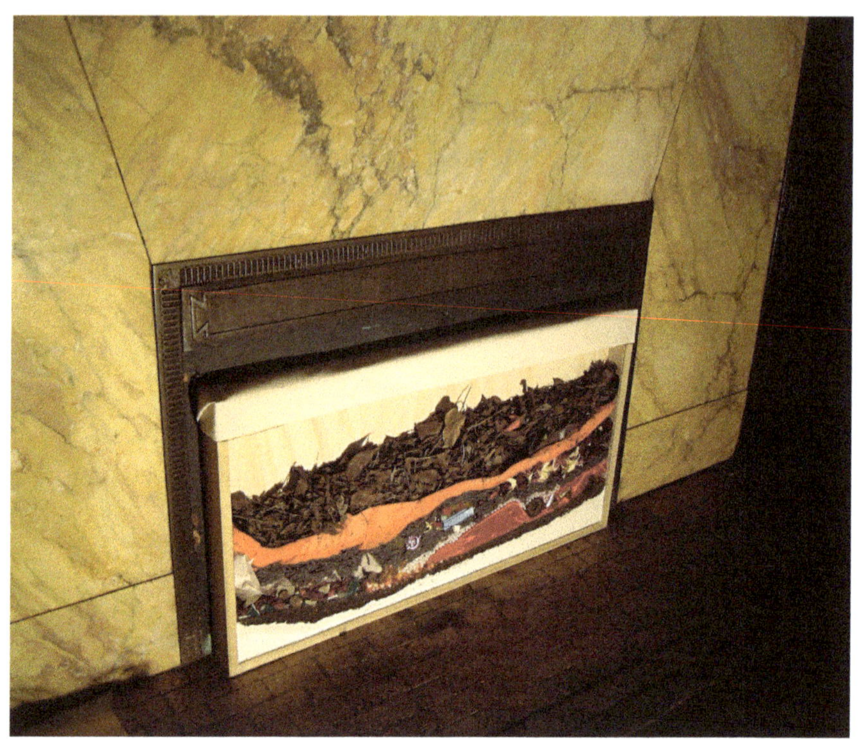

Lucie Matejkova, *Slice of Life*, 2008
cloth, eaves, lindenberries, buttons, found objects, ribbon, 2 x 3 feet x 4 inches
using the fireplace as a way to layer the history of the servants

It was built for John Farson. However he lived there only ten years, from 1897 to 1908, when Herbert Mills bought the house. Mills was an entrepreneur and innovator who made his fortune through the Mills Novelty Company. The firm designed and invented early vending machines. They also invented a Violano Virtuoso—a complex mechanized music machine. Mills was something of a character, known throughout the neighborhood for organizing bike parades and entertainments on the grounds as well as for his own exploits on bikes and roller skates.

In 1939, Mills sold the house to the Park District of Oak Park. This meant that the mansion, though built as an opulent private home, has been a public building for most of its history. It has been used to house meetings and activities for families, children and senior citizens. It has significant connections to the

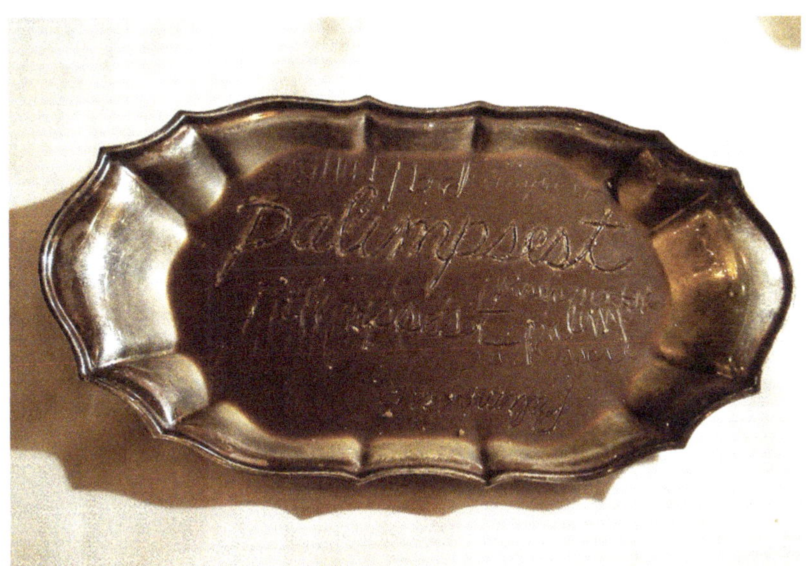

Rebecca Keller, *Palimpsest*, 2008
wax in vintage silver tray

Red Cross, including having served as a locale for Red Cross meetings and an RC office during WWII.

My students and I met with the director and staff of the house and the staff of the history society. We researched and discussed the ideas behind a historic house museum: At what date should the house be "frozen in time"? What is the purpose of such a house—should it be preserved as is, or kept alive and made relevant, or simply serve as a souvenir of the past for tourists to visit? What does it mean that this has served as a public resource for far longer than it was a private residence?

Our research led in several parallel directions, all of which could be accommodated within the exhibition. Several of the students/artists did work that re-imagined Mills in the house—either in the masculine privacy of his study, or as the public man roller-skating through the halls. In one of several activities that referenced the Red Cross, I organized a blood drive as well as a community bike drive with Working Bikes, a well-known biking nonprofit, commemorating the house's connection to biking and re-inscribing the public service aspect of the place.

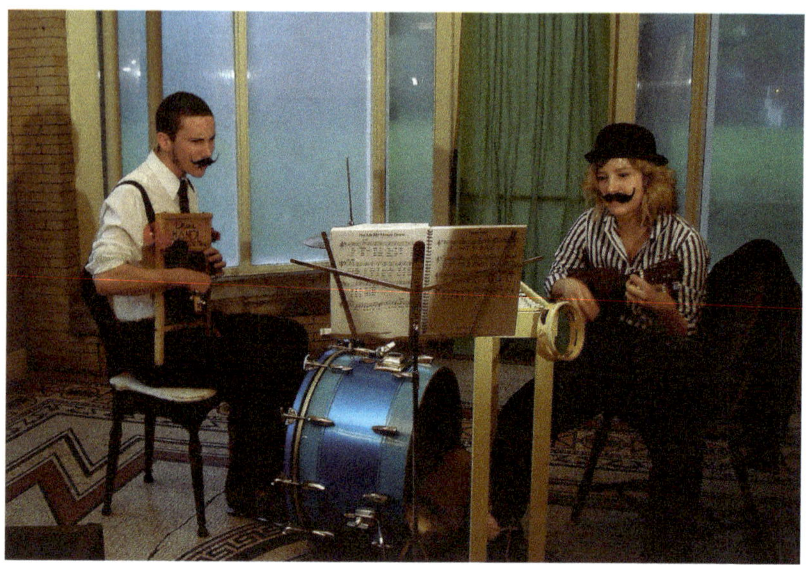

Dylan Jones and Marjorie Bailey, performance using handmade instruments and costumes, 2008
Jones and Bailey were fascinated by the history of musical performance in the house. Musicians as well as artists, they put together an old-timey performance, including making some of the instruments.

Students created musical performances for homemade instruments, referencing Mills's business and the fact that the Pleasant Home Foundation owned a violano virtuoso. One student addressed the problematics around the idea of restoration and preservation (How much should the evidence of years be erased? How much of the history is contained in the wear and tear?), by repairing chips in woodwork or a broken grating with brightly glazed porcelain. Another used the fireplace to create a fictive archeological site, with layered "samples" of imagined artifacts from each era of the house; another cast dishes for the butler's pantry of cinnamon, perfuming it with an aroma both homey and exotic. Other students keyed their work off stories of the original Mrs. Farson, an imposing figure who received visitors in formal dress, one at a time, as if for an audience; still others embroidered a tablecloth for the enormous custom-built dining room table.

My contribution to the exhibition addressed some of the meta-questions about the purpose and missions of house museums.

Referencing Maher's honeysuckle motif, I made a multi-part installation that used a live cutting from a hundred year old honeysuckle vine (courtesy of the Oak Park Conservatory), a dried section of the vine, and souvenir coins stamped with the honeysuckle motif. It was titled *Preserve, Alive, Remember*.

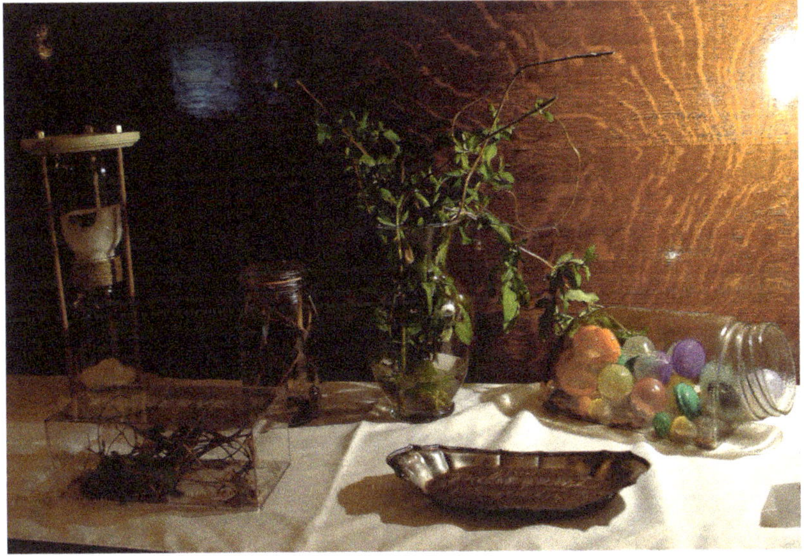

Rebecca Keller, *Preserve, Alive, Remember*, 2008
hourglass, museum collection case and bell jar, dried honeysuckle vine, vase, living vine, vintage cookie jar, souvenir coins stamped with honeysuckle, silver tray with wax, 6 x 4 feet

Preserve, Alive, Remember riffs on the honeysuckle motif used throughout the house to examine the role of historic sites. Are they meant to be forever locked in a rosy past for tourists; as living places, actively generating new ideas; or as aids to memory? This installation contained a cutting of a century-old honeysuckle vine, a dried section of the same vine, and a vintage cookie jar filled with vending machine 'bubbles' containing a souvenir coin stamped with a honeysuckle motif.

home for the histories

vince michael

Rebecca Keller has engaged, challenged, and energized the historic house museum through her artistic interventions in places like Glessner House in Chicago and Pleasant Home in Oak Park. At Glessner House she made visible the traditionally shielded lives of the domestic staff required to operate and maintain a large Victorian-era house. Servants' lives were illuminated by foregrounding their presence amidst an architecture that deliberately hid them. I was enthused by the project both because it offered another narrative to the "master narrative" of architecture and high society that had always been interpreted at Glessner House, and also because it was an artistic installation that gave us all a reason to re-visit the house.

The greatest challenge to historic house museums is no longer the explosion of the master narrative—many of the National

Trust's historic sites now foreground the contributions and lives of free and enslaved persons who made those sites function historically. The greatest challenge today is making those sites dynamic enough to require ongoing visitation, engagement, and involvement; to avoid not just the master narrative but the singular narrative that allows you to see an historic place, incorporate its lessons, and never return as long as you live.

This is why Keller's interventions are to be encouraged, expanded and promulgated. Her students' interventions at Pleasant Home provided a range of thematic and formal explorations of the site, each presenting a new perspective. I want that to happen at many sites, and to happen many times. The value of preserving a historic site is not that you save a particular history or narrative. The value is that you have a site of narrative that can be constantly re-engaged, re-interpreted, interrogated and re-understood.

As a historian, I know that our understanding of history is subject to constant regeneration, from within as new evidence emerges and from without, as our previous narratives are challenged and refreshed. We preserve these places because they are the stage for this re-examination, interrogation, and interpretation. As Keller says, the offer "the simultaneity of various histories embodied in a physical space, all at the same time." Installations like hers allow us to give voice to more and more of these histories, enhancing the vitality and relevance of these places to our society and communities.

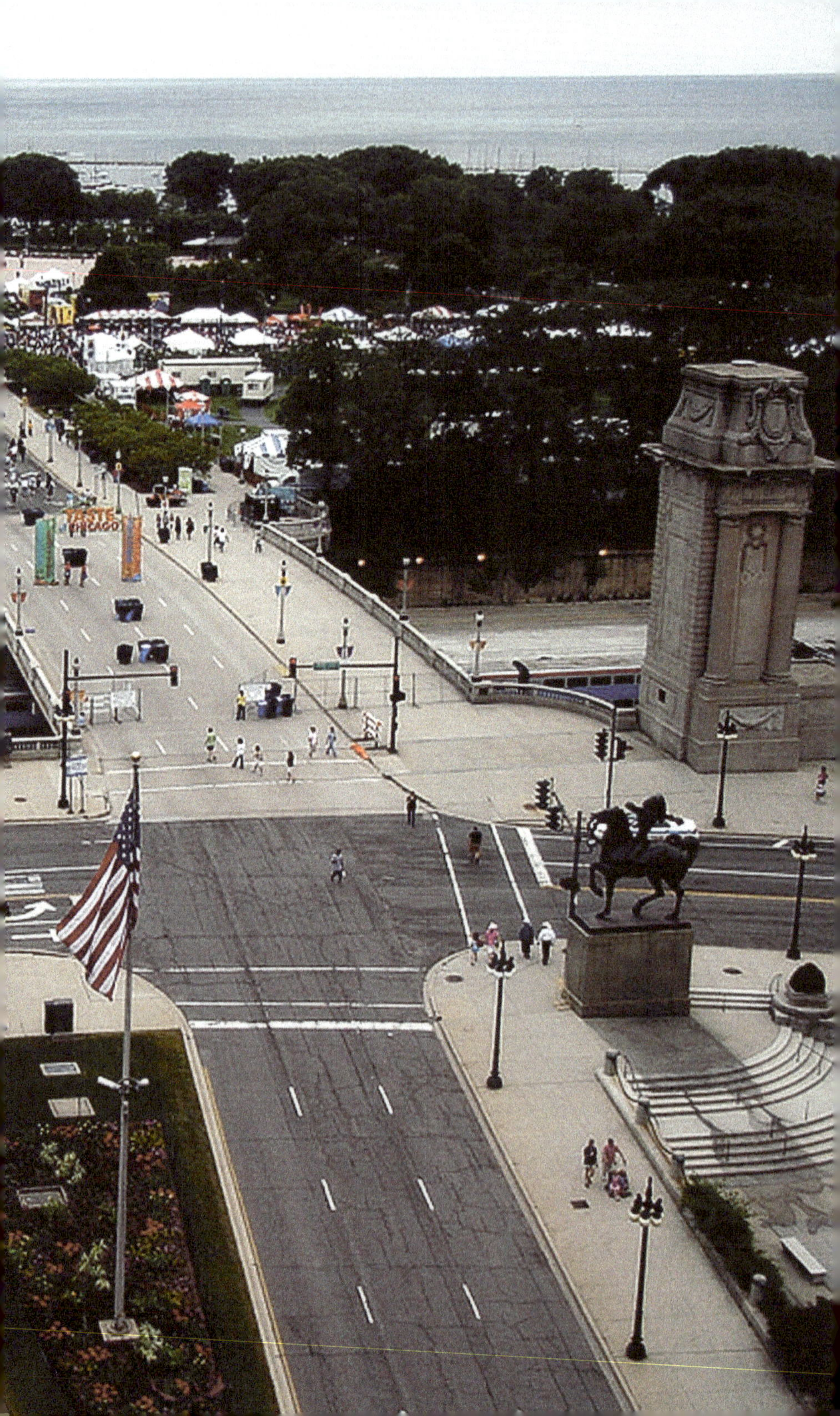
TASTE

excavating the loop 2009

rebecca keller

The centennial of Daniel Burnham's plan for the city of Chicago took place in 2009. Cultural institutions all over the city were hosting discussions and presentations about the anniversary. It seemed that for a class like Excavating History, not addressing Burnham's great achievement would be an almost willful omission. But the city is a collection of multiple, overlapping and very complex sites. Responding to the Burnham plan was both an enormous challenge and exciting opportunity.

The Chicago Cultural Center approved my request for residency in the Public Studio, and I committed to planning a class with the Loop itself as the center of our investigations. Additionally, we also received approval for the class to mount

left: Briana Schweizer, *It's About Time*, 2009

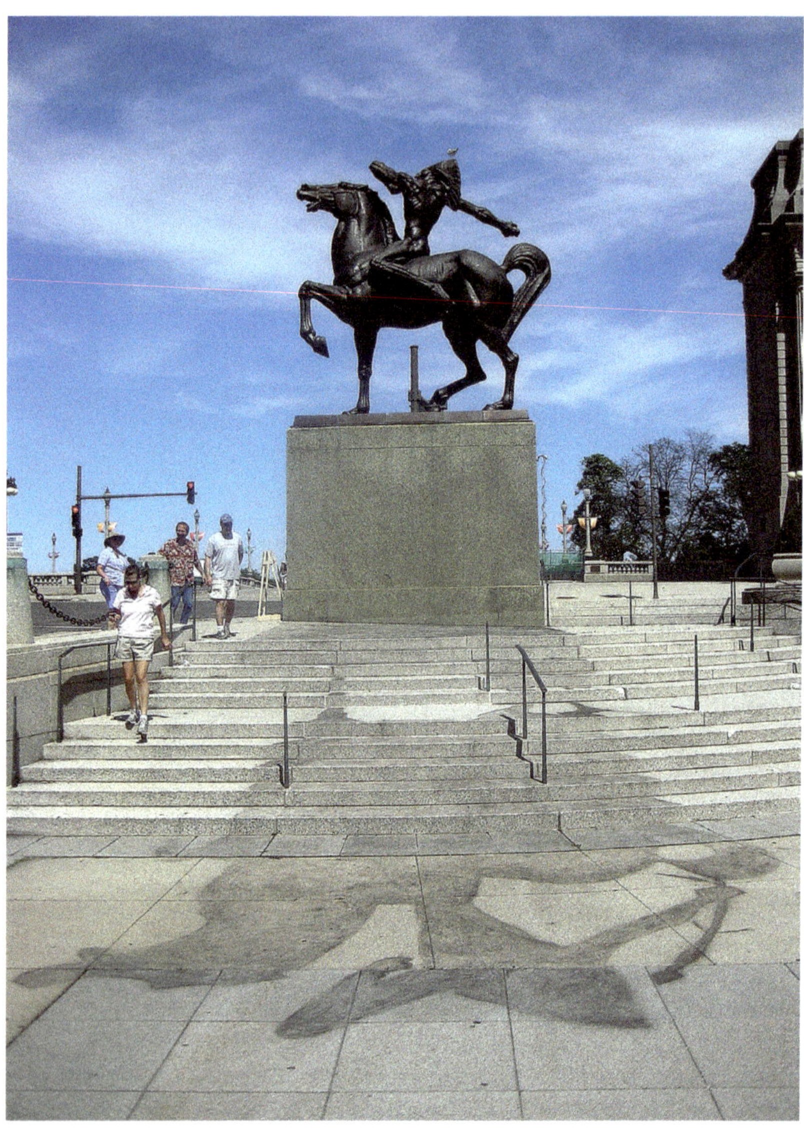

Briana Schweizer, *It's About Time*, 2009
outdoor drawing, charcoal, wood, 25 x 15 feet

a brief exhibition in the Sullivan center (formerly Carson Pirie Scott), Louis Sullivan's great building pictured in every architecture textbook.

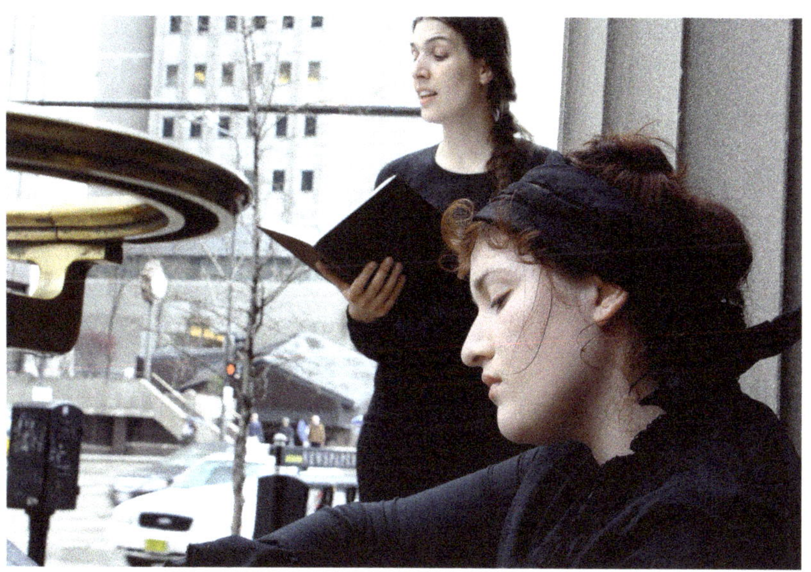

Elise Goldstein, Juliana Pivato, *Restoration*, 2009
gloves, wash line, music, wooden stands
On the steps of the Chicago Cultural Center, performing a work of healing and fund-raising for the Pilgrim Baptist Church.

We began by looking at *a city* as a phenomenon: students examined how the abstractions of plans and laws and surveyor's routes and maps are made manifest in thoroughfares and sidewalks and business districts. Several students analyzed the rhetoric of commemoration, including re-punctuating historic plaques to change their meaning, or recreating empty civic rituals. One "corrected" the shadow cast by two of Chicago's most famous statues, turning them into giant sundials that once a day aligned with their corrected versions in charcoal drawn "shadows" on the sidewalk.

Two other themes emerged: water, specifically the Chicago River, and fire.

One of the main features that drove the development of Chicago was the river, and several students took it as their research focus. One created a blog about the river, and interviewed people about their knowledge and attitudes toward it as they walked

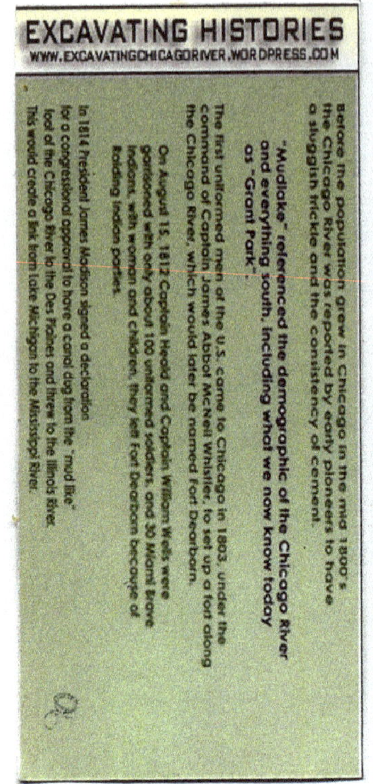

EXCAVATING HISTORIES
WWW.EXCAVATINGCHICAGORIVER.WORDPRESS.COM

Before the population grew in Chicago in the mid 1800's the Chicago River was reported by early pioneers to have a sluggish trickle and the consistency of cement.

"Mudlake" referenced the demographic of the Chicago River and everything south, including what we now know today as "Grant Park".

The first uniformed men of the U.S. came to Chicago in 1803, under the command of Captain James Abbot McNeil Whistler, to set up a fort along the Chicago River, which would later be named Fort Dearborn.

On August 15, 1812 Captain Heald and Captain William Wells were garrisoned with only about 100 uniformed soldiers, and 30 Miami Brave Indians, with woman and children, they left Fort Dearborn because of Raiding Indian parties.

In 1814 President James Madison signed a declaration for a congressional approval to have a canal dug from the "mud like" foot of the Chicago River to the Des Plaines and threw to the Illinois River. This would create a link from Lake Michigan to the Mississippi River.

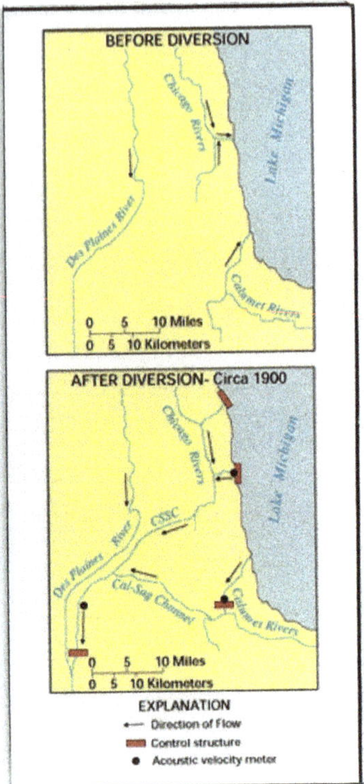

Matt Pudelek, *Chicago River Info Card*, 2009
Matt used these to engage people who stopped by the Cultural Center studio in a discussion about the history of the Chicago River and Fort Dearborn.

by the door of our studio. Another froze river water into ice which revealed text as it melted.

Chicago is, of course, a city shaped by fire. The great fire of 1871 is well known—indeed it was what prompted Burnham's plan and made it possible. Fittingly, one student marked places that had survived the fire with small hand-pulled woodcuts installed at the sites. She also continued her investigation/commemoration of the effects of fire and the need to rebuild by creating a public performance around a more recent 2006 fire at the Pilgrim Baptist Church--a building also designed by Sullivan. Pilgrim Baptist is credited with being where Thomas Dorsey invented Gospel music. Her performance/installation included the acapella singing of

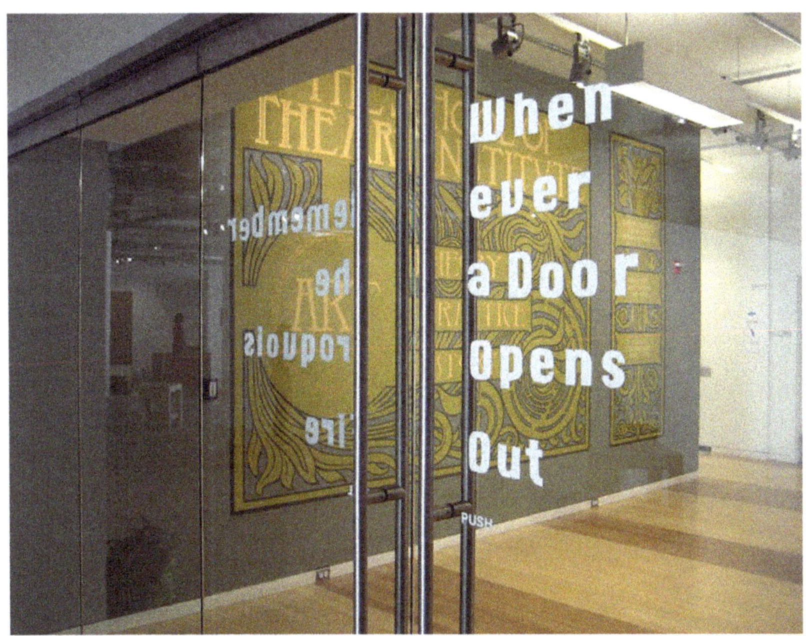

Rebecca Keller, *Performed Daily: A Living Memorial To The Iroquios Theater Fire*, 2009
vinyl text on door in Louis Sullivan Landmark Building, 2 x 4 feet
Keller's Installation at the Sullivan Center, referencing the international changes in building codes that resulted from the 1906 fire at a theater in Chicago, which left 600 people dead.

Dorsey's "Peace in the Valley" on the steps of the Cultural Center for several hours during rush hour one rainy afternoon.

The deadliest single building fire in United States history also happened in Chicago at the Iroquois Theater in December 1903. It took more than 600 lives. Many of the dead were found piled near exits. The doors had been built to open inward—impossible with panicked crowds pushing toward them. As a result, building codes around the world were changed. In response, I created *Performed Daily: a Living Memorial to the Iroquois Theater Fire*. For this piece, vinyl letters were placed on glass doors in the Sullivan gallery in such a way that half the phrase faced forward and half faced the other direction. Put together, the phrase read "Whenever a door opens out/I remember the Iroquois fire."

following spread: Elise Goldstein, Juliana Pivato, *Restoration*, 2009

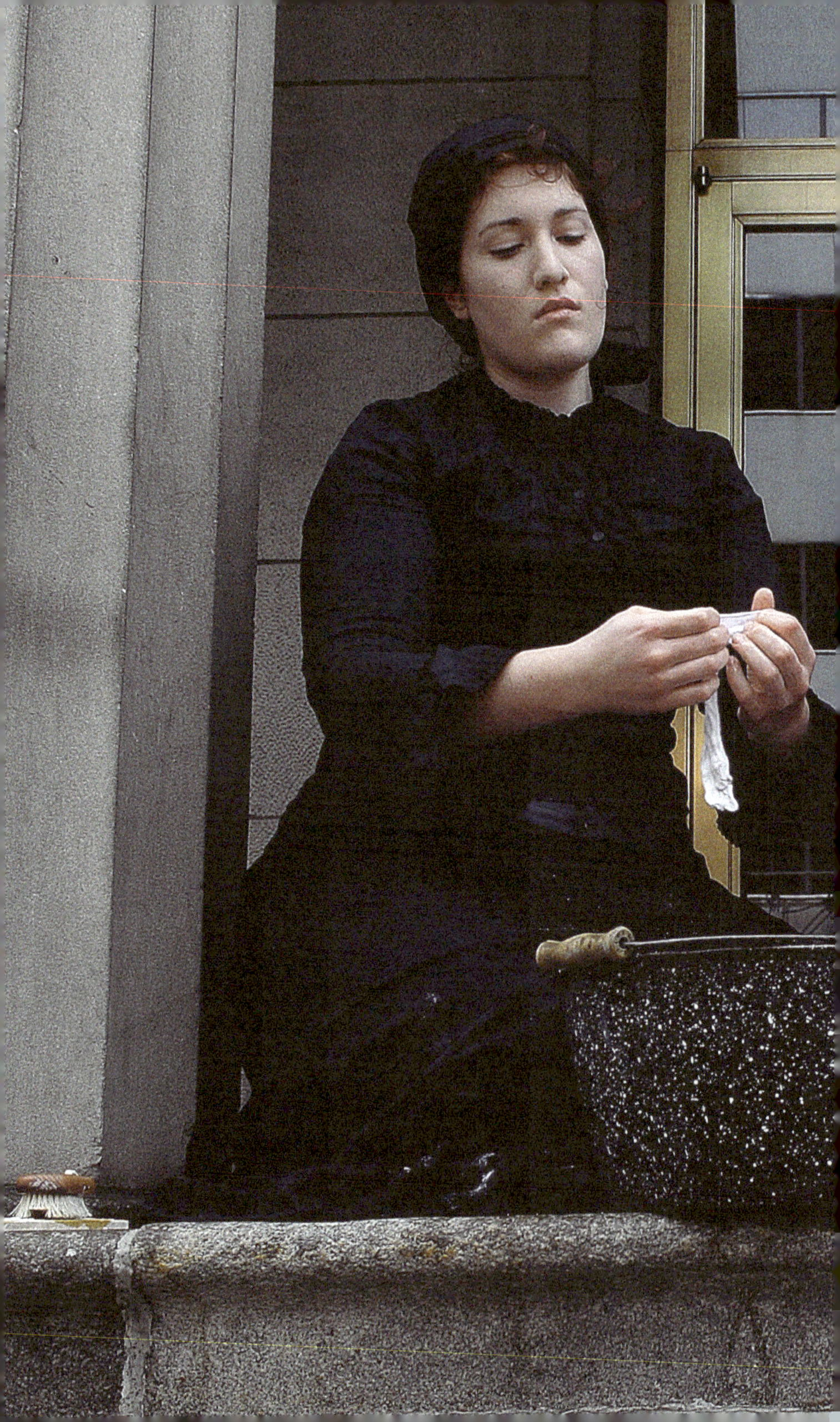

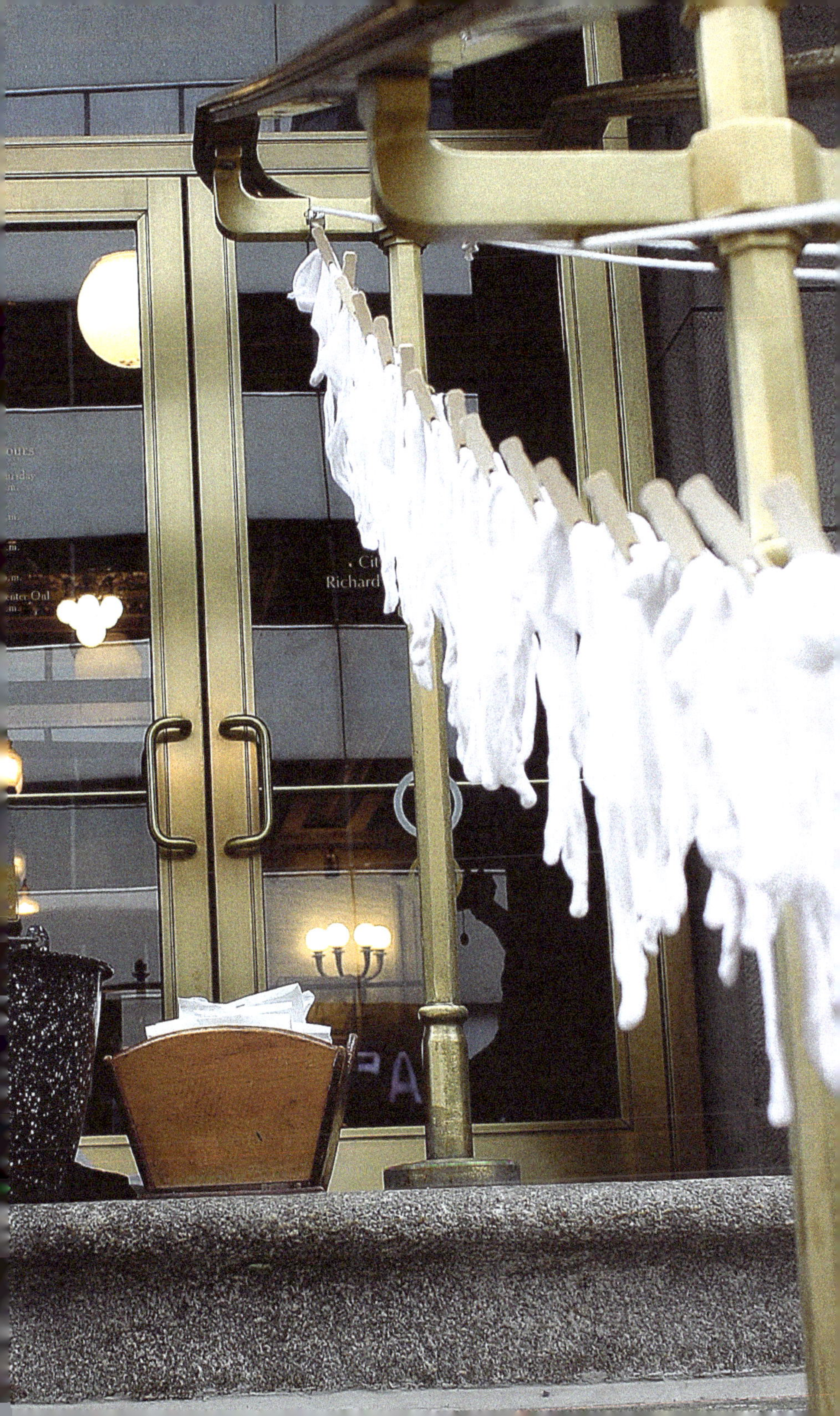
Richard

why excavate histories?

mary jane jacob

History needs to be excavated...not because it is the domain of archaeology where things must be dug up and then pieced together, as one imagines and interprets what was. History must also be excavated because some stories remain hidden or because new perspectives help us unearth other ways of seeing. This task is driven by the understanding that the lives of others must be remembered and rethought because the inroads and byways that enable us to remap history after a time both make it alive for us and make it right. So, it is true, history carries with it an agenda of justice—getting the story right.

Often in history there is more than one version, there are many ways of remembering, and some of these ways involve misremembering, which can also embody a real experience. This route, sometimes taken by art, can be more telling than facts alone. Having taken up this practice of looking at history as a curator, I can say that the artists I have engaged were not trying to be historians, but to work between fact and intuition to create an experience, thus engaging an audience in a way that could communicate across that time and geography. Their work helped bring us closer to the past. And sometimes the fictional (or not always fully factual) paths they followed in fabricating a project told more as they embodied the spirit of a time now gone.

A great author on experience, philosopher John Dewey—who also understood the power of art to tell stories—once wrote: "Art celebrates with peculiar intensity the moments in which the past reinforces the present and in which the future is a quickening of what now is."[1] And this brings me to the students who shared this experience of looking at history with Rebecca Keller. Grappling with histories foreign to their own experiences, they found ways to enter into incidents of the past that may at first seem remote, and bring them forward for themselves and for others.

Yet why excavate histories in a class? Dewey was a proponent of the "learning by doing" and he would have readily agreed that this was a great method for these artists and their audiences. Using the whole self—body and mind—is the best way to learn, he felt: integrating lessons into our very being and allowing ourselves to be realized through the act of learning. And I have no doubt that "Excavating History" at once brings history to the surface of experience and manifests those histories within us.

---

1. John Dewey, *Art as Experience* (New York: Penguin Group, 2005; originally published 1934), 17.

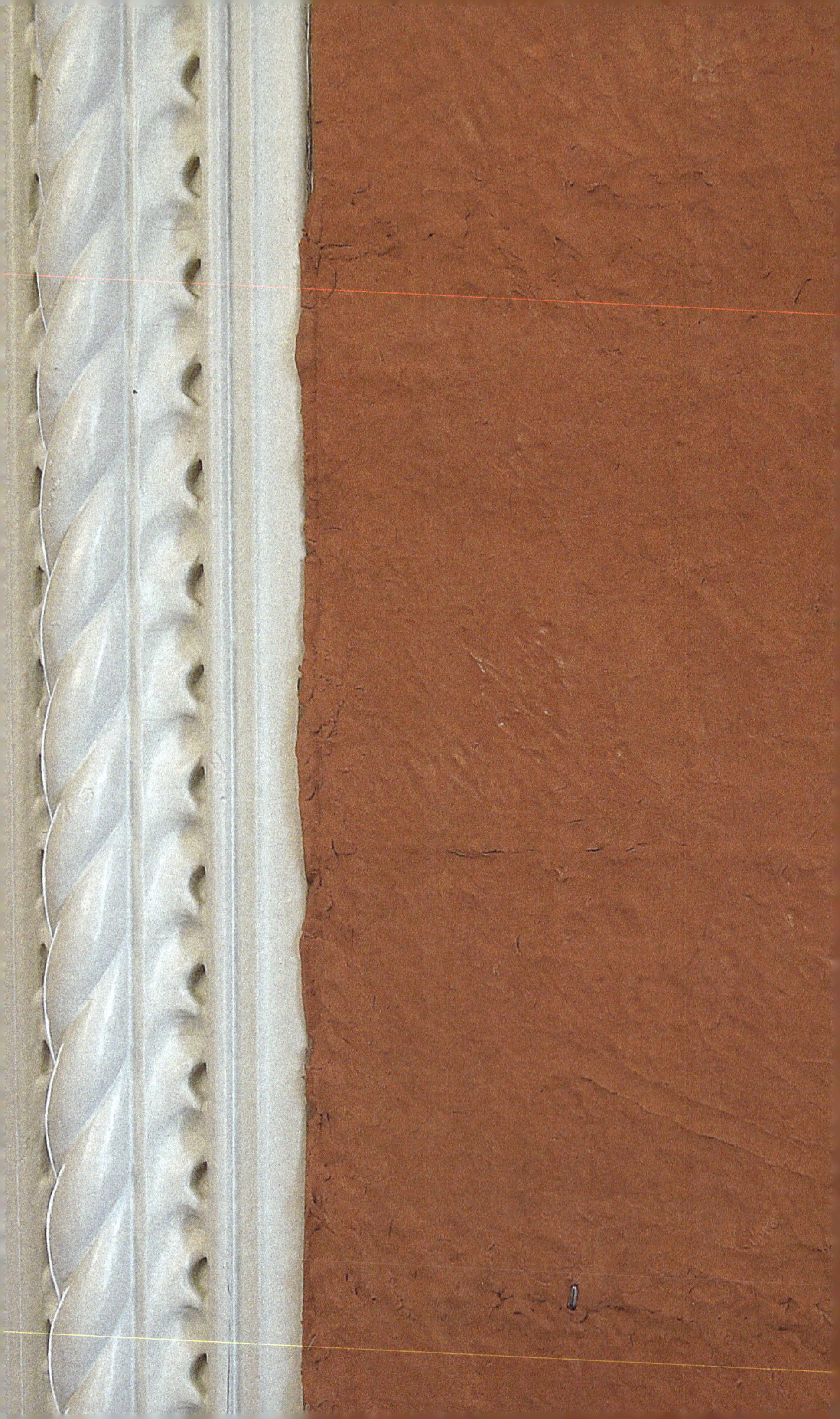

excavating hull-house 2010

rebecca keller

Jane Addams won the Nobel Peace prize in 1931 for her work at the Hull-House and for promoting peace abroad. She was among the first generation of women to attend college and, like others of this generation, felt strongly that she had something to offer society beyond stereotypical female roles. After touring Europe and discovering London's Toynbee Hall, a settlement house serving the residents of the city's east end, Addams and her friend Ellen Gates Starr founded a settlement house in Chicago's impoverished 19th ward, in 1889. The area was home to a diverse group of immigrants, and when the Hull-House Settlement opened, it helped to build community by offering classes in everything from ceramics to American citizenship. Other women and men from privileged backgrounds moved to

left: Rebecca Keller, *Fingerprint by Fingerprint* (detail), 2010
photo Emerson Granillo

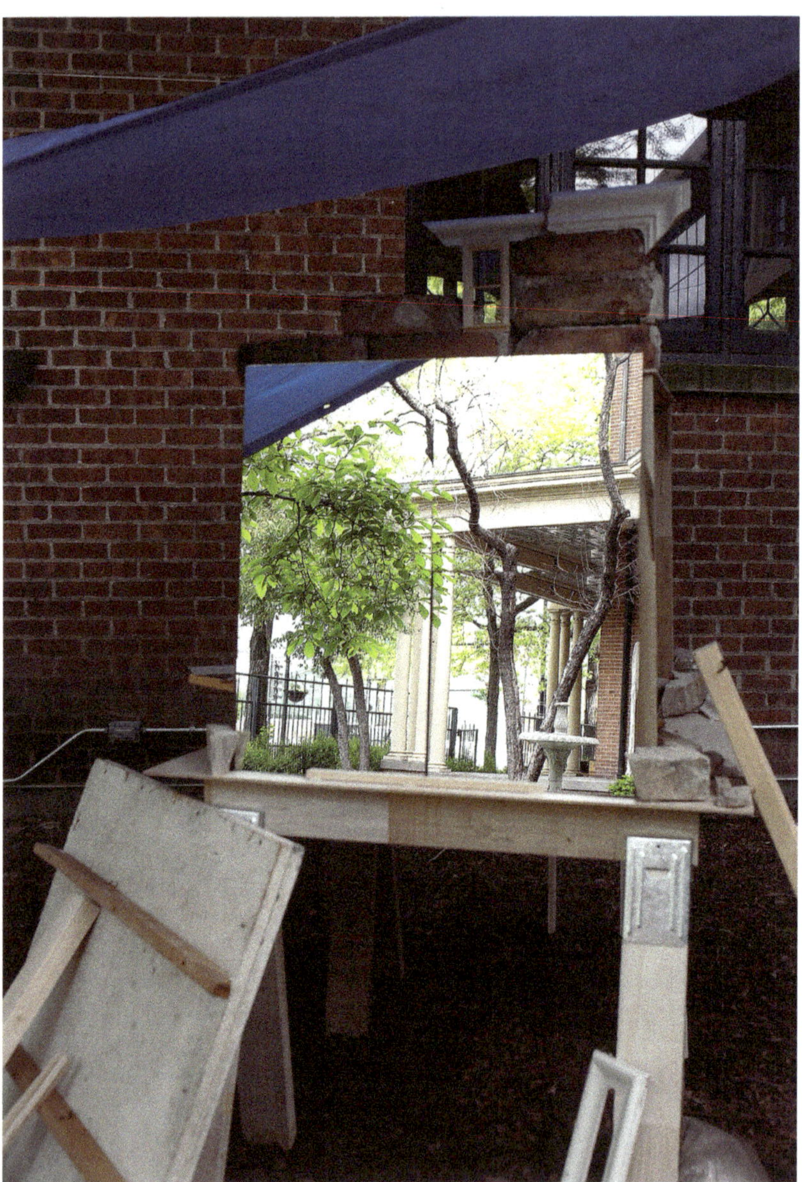

Cori Williams, *Tri-Remodeling Destruction*, 2010
construction materials, doll furniture, mirrors, tarp
photo Emerson Granillo

Hull House and volunteered their time. These residents advocated for labor reform, improved housing conditions, sex education in schools, public health improvement and also lobbied

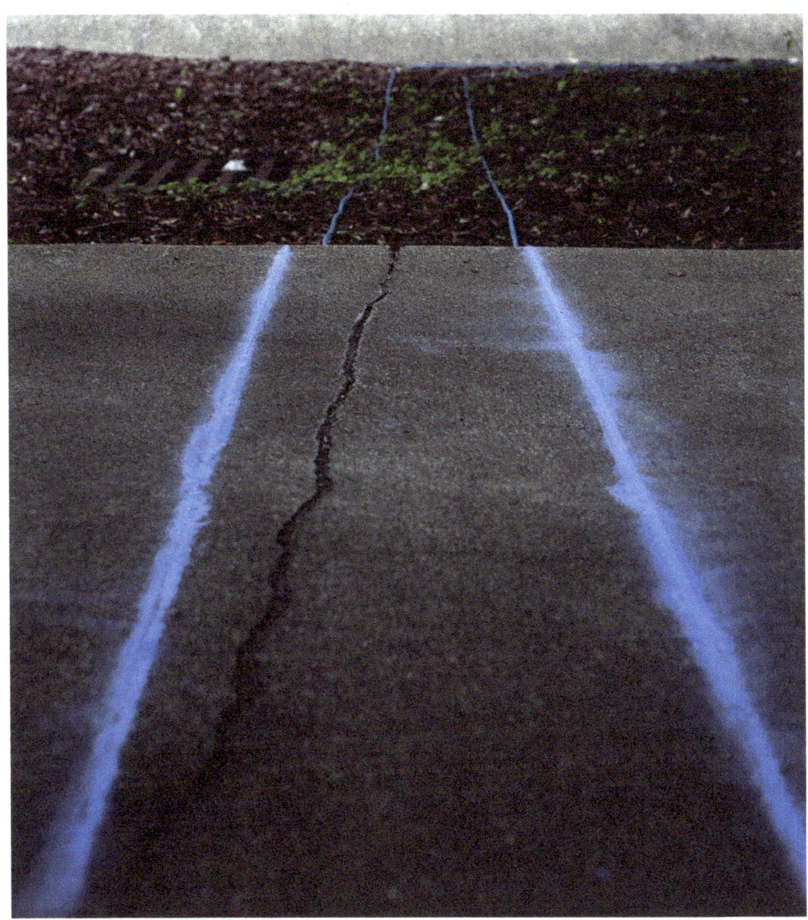

Liene Bosquê, *1963*, 2010
photo Emerson Granillo

for women's suffrage. The Hull House created a communal kitchen, established the idea of visiting nurses and free public playgrounds, and helped found the professions of social work and public health, as well as earning Addams the designation "The most dangerous woman in America."

The Jane Addams Hull-House Museum is her original home and settlement house, preserved as a national landmark and museum. Working with the Hull House was an enormous opportunity for the Excavating History class: in addition to the inspiring

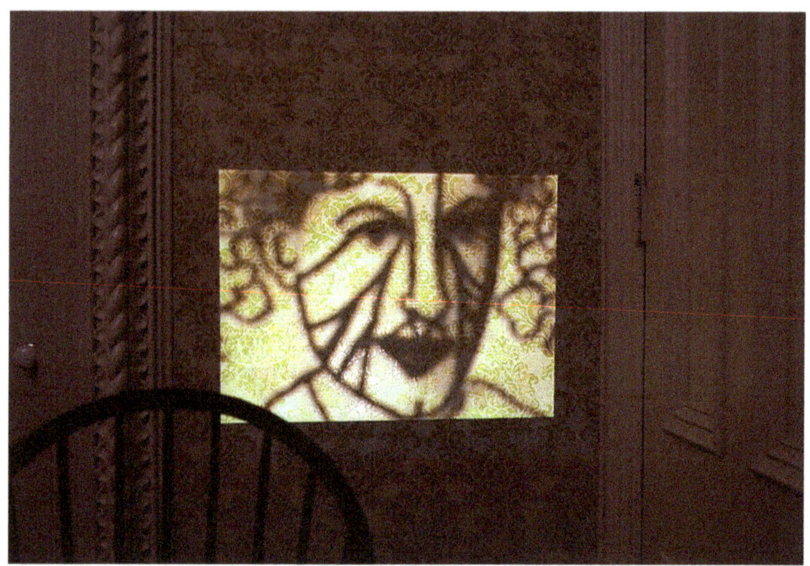

Sarah Legow, *The Yellow Wallpaper,* 2010
hand-drawn animation based on the story *The Yellow Wallpaper,* written by Charlotte Perkins Gilman, resident at Hull-House
photo Emerson Granillo

example of Jane Addams herself, there is a commitment on the part of the museum to continue Addam's legacy of meaningful contributions to society, and an openness to having that legacy be re-interpreted and re-engaged in new ways.

By sheer coincidence, the 2010 *Excavating History* class consisted of only women. Perhaps not coincidentally, they were pre-disposed toward a deep appreciation for the legacy of Jane Addams. The contemporary iterations of the work that Addams pursued: immigration policy, the politics of food and nutrition, labor, sexuality, and advocacy for civil rights, were all aspects of the exhibition that resulted.

Students were interested in the fact that the original Hull House Association comprised eleven buildings, most of which were torn down when the University of Illinois at Chicago was built (The university's graduate school of social work is named after Jane Addams). One student recreated the missing third floor of the house (removed during the 70s in a "restoration") and another, using chalk, cord and stencils, marked the boundaries, entrances, exits, purposes and dates of every building that had been in the complex, tracing on the ground the literal footprint of the scope of Addams's work.

Addams did not pursue her work alone: the Hull House drew men and women who became residents and helped advance her vision. One of the students did a piece that activated this history through the use of hundreds of house keys attached to embroidered tags, and another created an animation based on the work of Charlotte Perkins Gilman, the author of the proto-feminist classic *The Yellow Wallpaper*, and briefly a resident at Hull House.

In addition to Addams the public figure, we were interested in Jane Addams the woman: friend, mentor, daughter, and writer—a woman whose public work and professional mentorship profoundly touched many lives, but who experienced loneliness, frustration and sadness, and who was perhaps prevented from expressing her own needs because of her public profile.

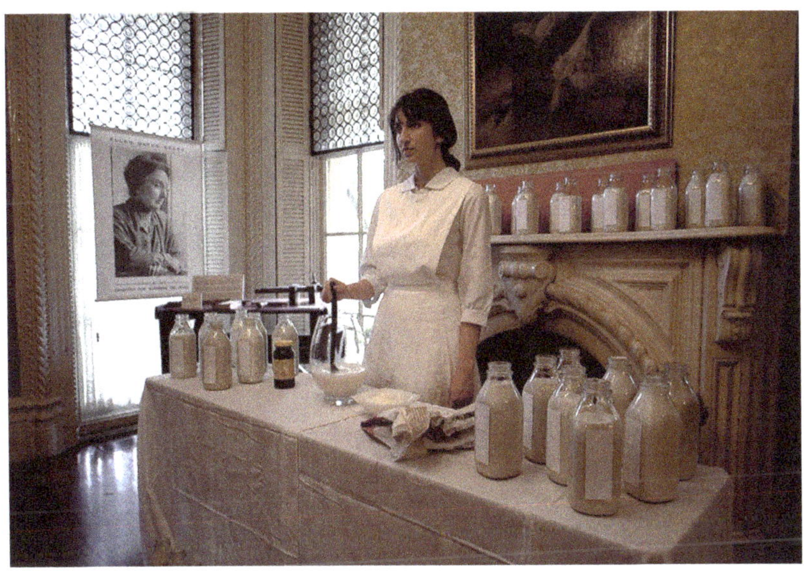

Maral Hashemi, *Elixir of life*, 2010
photo Emerson Granillo

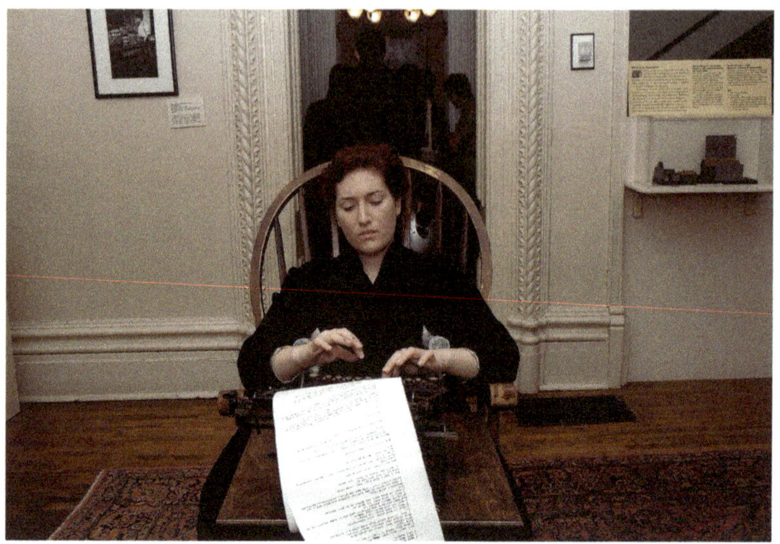

Elise Goldstein, *The Ink Well* (detail), 2010
installation view in the parlor of the Hull-House Museum
photo Emerson Granillo

We imagined her emotional life as a mentor and nurturer as well as a person who doubtless needed support and love. One student created a performance in which, seated in a rocking chair in Addams's parlor, she composed a "stream-of-consciousness" letter of comfort: "To Jane." The paper fell from the vintage machine, stretched across the floor and curled into the fireplace, some feet away. When visitors approached they read the letter and also became aware of a gentle wheezing sound. Barely visible through the altered dress the student wore, a breast pump methodically pulled at her nipples—a moving metaphor to Addam's life of offering nurturance and comfort to the point of pain and self-sacrifice.

Several students created work about immigration, using tools as diverse as video, embroidery, oral history, and a zoetrope powered by an altered treadle sewing machine. Another reenacted the difficult journey of immigrant women by dragging a suitcase filled with paving bricks from the site of the former train station, a mile away, to Hull House, where she created a memorial installation using the suitcase, paving stones from the original

Halsted street, and photos. One arresting installation referred to the dumping of bad milk in the 19th ward by deploying dozens of vintage milk bottles filled with plaster and labeled "white poison" in dozens of languages.

Jane Addams was convinced of the importance of immigrants' handicraft traditions, feeling that connections to culture were as necessary as food and shelter to people's sense of well-being. For my contribution to the exhibition I covered entire walls of her parlor with terra cotta, painstakingly rubbing it (with the help of collaborators) into wall-sized panels which were then used to line the rooms. The piece referenced collective labor, the Hull House history of ceramics, and also the fact that the original walls were the color of terra cotta. The clay remained soft, allowing all who visited to "leave their mark."

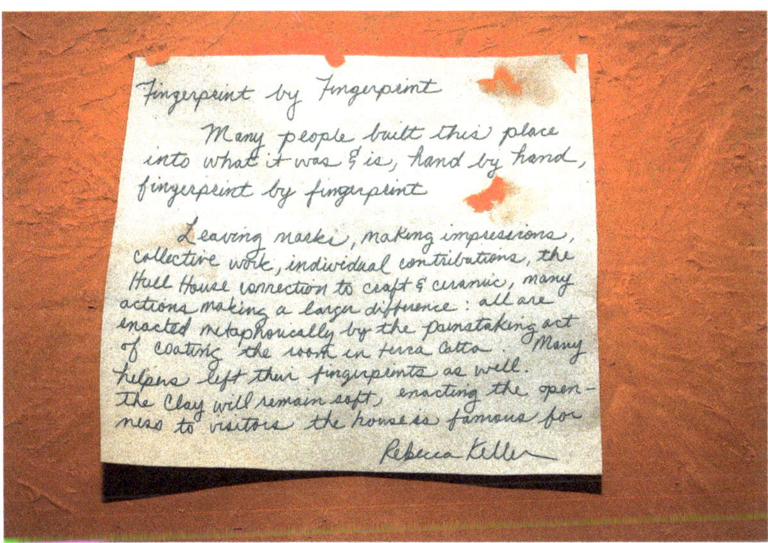

Fingerprint by Fingerprint

Many people built this place into what it was & is, hand by hand, fingerprint by fingerprint

Leaving marks, making impressions, collective work, individual contributions, the Hull House connection to craft & ceramic, many actions making a larger difference: all are enacted metaphorically by the painstaking act of coating the room in terra cotta. Many helpers left their fingerprints as well. The clay will remain soft, enacting the openness to visitors the house is famous for

Rebecca Keller

Rebecca Keller, *Fingerprint by Fingerprint* (detail), 2010
photo Emerson Granillo

) head?

gler
about this

For Future Surgeries:

- marionette type attachment
- nano surgeries in the brain (
  vs. with fat, simulate [illegible]
- remote surgeries (maybe in m[illegible]
- surgeon as night watchman

Headache pills:
Skullcap, valerian, rosemary, cham[illegible]
equal parts powdered herbs, blend [illegible]

Mandrake, henbane, Datura metel

Angelica dahurica
wolfsbane
Lingusticum wallichii or Szech[illegible]
Angelica sinensis or "female gin[illegible]
Chinese monkshood
Jimson weed
[illegible]

welcoming museum takeovers

(or, what to expect when you're expecting the unexpected)

lisa junkin

"expect the unexpected."

—hyde park art center, 2006

In 2006, the Hyde Park Art Center (HPAC), a center for contemporary art located on the south side of Chicago, debuted its new facility with an exhibit called *Takeover.* With a motto, "expect the unexpected" and public affirmation that "the new Art Center will be a laboratory for experimental art and ideas," HPAC invited 39 artists to create artwork that would literally take over the building—from galleries and offices to the bathrooms and even the roof. Works were site-specific and

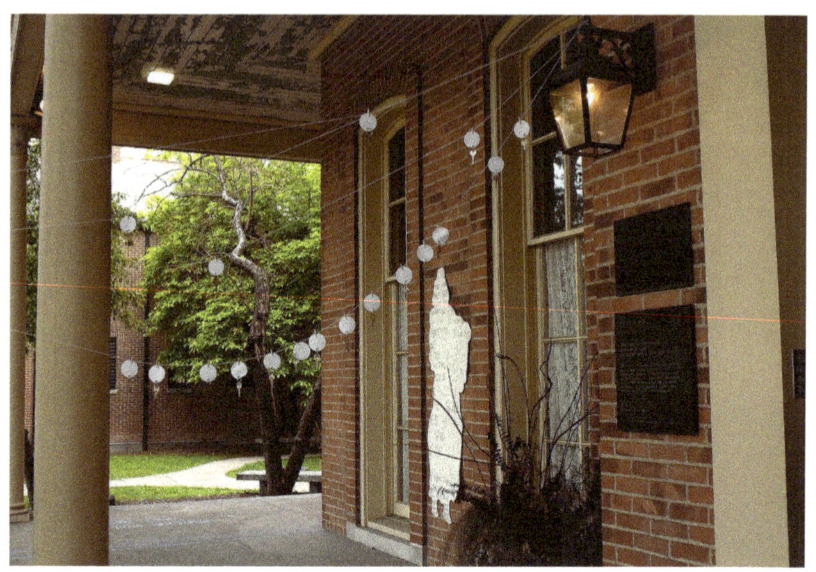

Allison Jenetopulos, *Welcome Home*, 2010
keys, embroidered linen tags, handmade table, labels, line, clothespins
Jenetpulos created a key for each resident who had ever stayed at Hull House. Visitors were invited to take a key upon entering, and hang it on the line when they left.

responded to their immediate environment, the larger neighborhood, and HPAC's history.[1]

After seeing that exhibit, I often found myself returning to the idea of a "takeover" in cultural spaces like art centers, libraries, and museums. In HPAC's exhibit, contemporary art functioned as an innovative way to expand the uses of a cultural institution—to help visitors begin to "expect the unexpected" and to engage museums in new ways. At the same time, aspects of the *Takeover* exhibit felt safe—even expected—in a contemporary art center. I began to wonder about what further takeovers might look like. What does it mean to take over a cultural space? Are there other examples of what a takeover might look like? How might institutions welcome a takeover? Could other kinds of museums give their spaces over to artists? To the public?

1. "2006 exhibitions: Takeover," Hyde Park Art Center, accessed June 6, 2011, http://www.hydeparkart.org/exhibitions/2006/04/takeover.php

In fact, a takeover of sorts is well underway, a cultural revolution in which communities reassert their need for museums and vice versa. In the last 25 years, multiple publics have advanced the takeover of cultural institutions by advocating for expanded and more democratic forms of preservation and exhibitions. For example, LGBTQ history is beginning to be highlighted in museum exhibits. Complex narratives of difference and oppression are surfacing where stories of the dominant culture were once the only focus. Women and artists of color are asked to particpate in more exhibitions than ever before. In some cases, as in the National Museum of Mexican Art and the National Museum of the American Indian, communities have founded their own museums in order to share their own stories.[2] In an environment where museums resemble forums more than temples, the potential is strong for takeovers to highlight their ability to reveal hidden narratives and for publics to build community and engage in civic dialogue.

taking over the historic house

I was fortunate to be able to experiment with a contemporary art takeover at the Jane Addams Hull-House Museum (JAHHM), an historic house museum dedicated to the life and work of America's first woman to win the Nobel Peace Prize. It is an institution that has previously worked to take up the democratization of museums by exploring untold narratives at our site. Our staff is inspired by the writings of scholars and museum

2. See Karen Mary Davalos, *Exhibiting Mestizaje: Mexican (American) Museums in the Diaspora* (Albuquerque: University of New Mexico Press, 2006); Douglas Evelyn, "The Smithsonian's National Museum of the American Indian: An International Institution of Living Cultures," *The Public Historian* 28:2 (2006): 51-56; Amy K. Levin (ed.), *Gender, Sexuality, and Museums: A Routledge Reader* (New York: Routledge, 2010); Klaus Müller, "Invisible Visitors: Museums and the Gay and Lesbian Community," *Museum News*, September/October 2001.

professionals such as Elaine Heumann Gurian and Stephen Weil[3], who have pushed museums to rethink their audience, mission, and boundaries. As a result, the museum seeks to make connections between past and present on social justice topics including immigration, labor, education, the arts, women's rights, and peace.

In the past four years, the Hull-House Museum has greatly expanded its public programs to focus on contemporary issues of social justice. A program called Re-thinking Soup allows visitors to feed their minds with conversations on food and justice while eating organic, locally made soup. A documentary film series explores sexuality and questions of consent, freedom, and social stigmas. The Conversations on Peace and Justice program invites contemporary activists and scholars to discuss the critical issues of our time. But for all the changes to the museum's public programming, the museum's permanent exhibit had remained largely untouched.[4] Our staff was therefore delighted when artist-teacher Rebecca Keller proposed that her Excavating History class from the School of the Art Institute of Chicago (SAIC) come to research Hull-House history and create a responsive, site-specific art exhibit.

Many contemporary art practices are fluid, relational, and research-oriented, making them an ideal match for museums interested in opening their collections and exhibitions to new players and ideas.[5] Still, the visions of artists working in an

---

3. Elaine Heumann Gurian, *Civilizing the Museum: The Collected Writings of Elaine Heumann Gurian* (New York: Routledge, 2006); Stephen Weil, *A Cabinet of Curiosities: Inquiries into Museums and their Prospects* (Washington and London: Smithsonian Institution Press, 1995).

4. The museum has since undergone a full renovation and now features a new permanent exhibit.

5. See Shannon Jackson, *Social Works: Performing Art, Supporting Publics* (New York, Routledge, 2011) and Nicolas Bourriaud, *Relational Aesthetics* (Dijon: Les Presses du Reel, 2002).

historical space can be intimidating to institutions that seek to maintain their own visions and exhibit objectives. I knew there would be a number of hurdles to jump for the exhibit to be a success, and that JAHHM would need to rethink some traditional museum practices in order to feel comfortable in allowing the takeover. But here was a radical opportunity for a historic house museum to make way for new interpretations—and possibly new critiques.

This kind of creative takeover within a museum has, of course, been influenced by artist Fred Wilson, whose curatorial-art practice and collaboration with the Maryland Historical Society and the Contemporary Museum was pivotal in shaping the idea of a meaningful intervention within a historical site. In 1992-3, Wilson was given an opportunity to re-curate the collection of the Maryland Historical Society as an artist in residence. His exhibit, *Mining the Museum*, unearthed a number of artifacts that had remained in storage for decades and exposed jarring contradictions that exist in history and museums, such as valuing the handiwork of white artisans while ignoring that of slaves. According to a report written by Americans for the Arts which provided support for *Mining the Museum*, the exhibit redefined the role of historical societies and museums and transformed the site's relationship with the African American community, a public that is now regularly represented within the museum's walls.[6]

Yet, there is still work to be done. Nearly 20 years after *Mining the Museum*, hardly any historical societies and historic house museums have introduced contemporary art into their sites as a way of expanding their narratives and audience. Some might argue that "It's been done," but I propose that Wilson's approach was only one format for a successful artist takeover. Curator Maurice Berger notes that Wilson's work "is so much

---

6. "Animating Democracy: Maryland Historical Society," Americans for the Arts, accessed June 6, 2011, http://www.artsusa.org/animatingdemocracy/labs/lab_055.asp

about what's absent, what's lost. He sees the museum as a kind of ruin. He opens up a wound and exposes areas that are hidden."[7] Entering into the Excavating History project, I expected the artists to provide a Wilson-esque critique of our history, exposing areas of racism, sexism, or other areas that the museum had neglected. But by and large, the work in the exhibit, ultimately titled *Messing with Jane*, did *not* mess with her so much as it celebrated and reinterpreted the history of the settlement with loving care. Certainly there is still room for the kind of critical examination that Wilson provided to the Maryland Historical Society, but often, museums are beginning to present more critical perspectives of their own volition. Therefore, I believe that other aesthetics and intellectual priorities for cultural takeovers can be developed, but they will not be revealed until other sites begin to explore and experiment with contemporary art.

As a contribution to the future of museum takeovers and my hope that many more historic house museums will look to contemporary art to revitalize their sites, I would like to offer some thoughts about the lessons I learned in my collaboration with Keller and the SAIC artist-students. These thoughts are particularly relevant to historic house museums, but will also be instructive to other cultural institutions. I hope to give readers a sense of what to expect when inviting similar collaborations to the historic sites, though I realize that part of the joy and excitement of this kind of project is the unexpected.

takeovers are a reason to return

It is no surprise that historic house museums are facing serious attrition of their audiences. The recent economic recession has brought about the shuttering of many historic houses, but the issue of lost patronage extends beyond the current financial climate. Although more Americans visit museums than ever before, historic house museums are some of the last to consider the changing needs of 21st century audiences. Gerald George,

---

7. Phoebe Hoban, "The Shock of the Familiar," *New York*, July 28, 2003. http://nymag.com/nymetro/arts/features/n_9014/

former director of the American Association for State and Local History, wrote in 2002:

> In the increasing competition for visitors, members, and financial support, many, if not most, historic sites are struggling for survival, and the quality of preservation and maintenance of many such sites has declined precipitously. In addition, the quality and appeal of the traditional historic house museum interpretation does not successfully compete with other contemporary sources of educational leisure time activities. Is it time for new models, new standards, or new approaches?[8]

The general public tends to hold a belief that historic houses contain static content, material that can be grasped within one visit to the site. Often, they are right. Exhibits in most historic house museums rarely change, staff is stretched thin and often do not have professional resources, and museum funding never meets the manifold needs of a site. For these reasons, recent trends to make museums more participatory, more relevant to contemporary and diverse audiences, and more central in the life of the community have been slow to catch on in historic houses.[9] The introduction of contemporary art into the historic house museum offers a way to engage these new practices which will encourage repeat visitors as a result. In fact, contemporary art might be the most practical way for an historic house museum to expand its reach; funding sources for temporary art exhibits might be more available than funding for permanent exhibitions, and much of the labor of creating the exhibit (though certainly not all, as I can attest) would come from the artists, not the museum staff.

---

8. Gerald George, "Historic House Museum Malaise: A Conference Considers What's Wrong, *History News,* (Autumn, 2002).

9. Of course, there are historic house museums that continue to experiment with and redefine what a 21st century museum should look like. See for example public programs at Harriet Beecher Stowe Center and interpretation at the Lower East Side Tenement Museum.

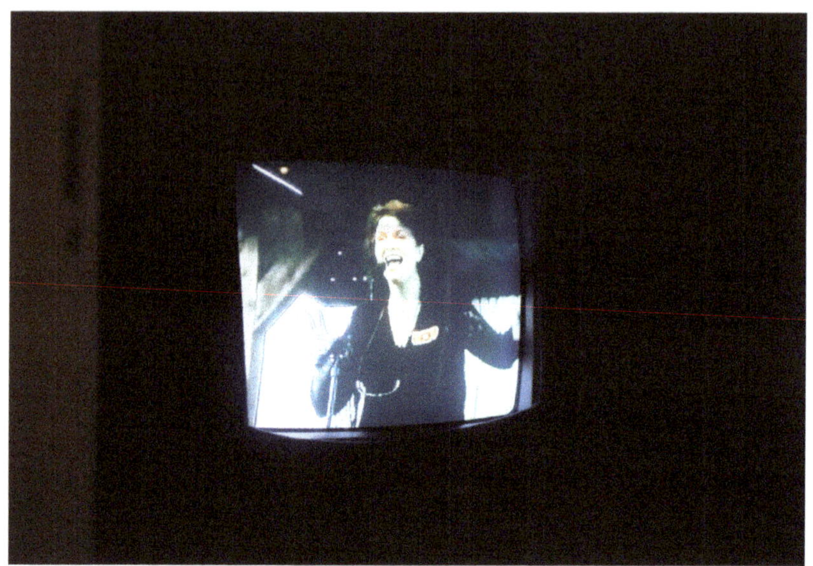

Rebecca Hernandez, *E Pluribus Unum/Ethnopaulism*, 2010
video installation

One of the ways in which *Messing with Jane* bolstered the efforts of JAHHM was by interpreting content that the museum did not have an opportunity to include in its permanent exhibitions, thereby offering visitors a reason to return. For example, some pieces offered content that had not been prioritized by the museum's staff. Sarah Legow's installation *Woman in the Wallpaper* freely adapted Charlotte Perkins Gilman's short story *The Yellow Wallpaper* in a site-specific animation projected onto yellow wallpaper in the back parlor of the Hull home. Gilman, though she visited Hull-House for a short time, is not a central figure at the Settlement. Although *The Yellow Wallpaper* resonates strongly in a space like Hull-House, the relationship between Gilman and Hull-House had not been made clear in any exhibitions until Leglow revealed the connection in a lovely and whimsical piece.

Other artwork made direct connections between the past and the present. Rebecca Hernandez created a piece of video art called *E pluribus unum, ethnophaulism*, which was installed within the house's original steel-walled safe. Referencing contemporary immigration, the piece used footage taken from an anti-"illegal" immigration speech but replaced the language with Morse code, signaling the increasingly coded language of these political activists. Historic house museums are rarely able to incorporate contemporary content into their exhibits, but here art offered an intriguing response to the current national rhetoric.

For the museum staff, these thoughtfully rendered works felt like a breath of fresh air. Though Hull-House history is broad, the staff is forced to limit our exhibitions by time period and content themes. In the ongoing debate over the role of objects in museums, artifacts are often falsely placed in opposition with ideas, and museums sometimes foolishly take sides against one or the other.[10] But if museums accept that they are about *both* objects and ideas, then an exhibit doesn't necessarily have to be limited by the scope of a collection. Innovative curating can help to fill in the gaps, and contemporary art provides a rich exploration of other modes of interpretation.

takeovers support new forms of learning

One of the most noticeable effects of the artwork in *Messing with Jane* was the visceral and lasting impression it had on audiences. Certainly there are artifacts that carry deep personal and emotional value, such as the thousands of shoes at Auschwitz or the Greensboro Lunch Counter, on view at the National Museum of American History, or for many of our visitors, Jane Addams' Nobel Peace prize. But when an artifact doesn't exist, or when its form doesn't carry the weight of its history, art can offer a more poignant way of understanding an historical moment.

Elise Goldstein's performance and installation *The Ink Well* offered an intimate response to the work of Jane Addams. In this performance and installation, Goldstein wrote an improvised letter to Addams as a means of connecting personally with this national hero. During the performance, Goldstein wore an antique black dress and working breast pumps while sitting in

10. Elaine Heumann Gurian, "What Is the Object of This Exercise? A Meandering Exploration of the Many Meanings of Objects in Museums," *Daedalus* 128:3, (Summer, 1999), 163-183.

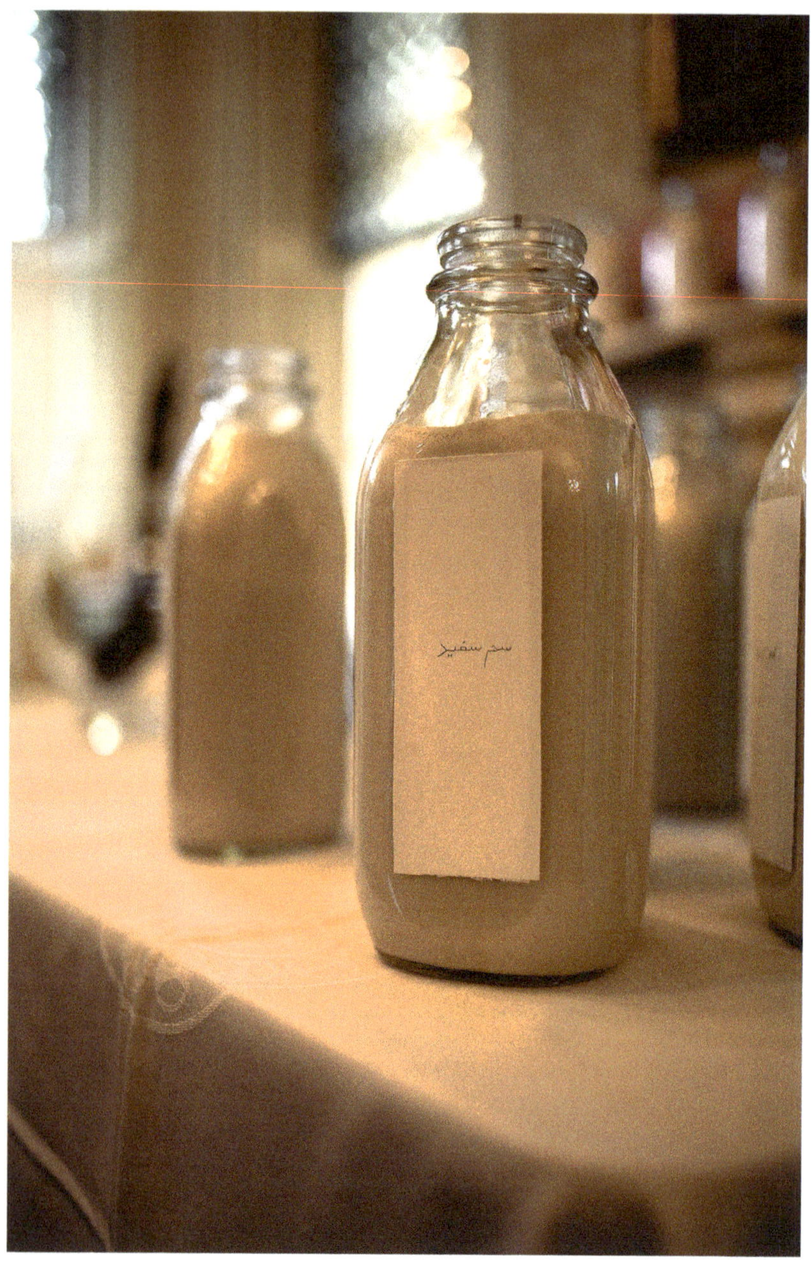

Maral Hashemi, *Elixir of life* (detail), 2010

a rocking chair. The letter, which was written on a typewriter equipped with one long roll of paper, extended at least 6 feet in length. Though the piece was confusing to some, the genuine honesty of the letter and the endurance aspect of the two-hour performance revealed in raw form some of the emotions that our visitors feel upon walking through the doors of Hull-House and encountering the spirit of Jane Addams. Though Goldstein may not have realized it, intense feelings of wonder, inspiration, and inadequacy have all been expressed by visitors to JAHHM. *The Ink Well* gave voice and form to those emotions.

Elixer of Life was an installation and performance by Maral Hashemi that excavated the history of swill milk and food adulteration in the Hull-House neighborhood, a practice that sometimes resulted in the deaths of infants. Addams responded to the issue directly, opening a pure milk station that by 1906 sold over 63,000 bottles of milk per year.[11] At the exhibit opening, Hashemi, dressed in a white nurse's uniform, ladled a white liquid from a glass bowl. She asked visitors if they would like a glass of milk, though one look at the raw materials that had been added to it, including molasses, plaster, and borax, discouraged visitors immediately. Hashemi surrounded the room with milk bottles with labels that read "white poison" in different languages, over 100 in all. The glass bottles had been filled with liquid plaster, which meant that as the plaster cured, the bottles cracked and fissured.

Our educators were so moved by this piece that they began to incorporate it into many of their tours for student groups. Here was an arresting story, never before told within the walls of the museum, that spoke volumes about the needs of the community and Hull-House's commitment to their improvement. Through Hashemi's piece, the story of adulterated milk could be taught effectively to students of all ages. The artwork didn't depend on specific knowledge of facts and dates, but instead relied on the humanity of the visitors and their sense

11. Jacqueline Wolf, *Don't Kill Your Baby: Public Health and the Decline of Breastfeeding in the Nineteenth and Twentieth Centuries* (Columbus: Ohio State University Press, 2001).

of outrage at the violation of something as basic as the right to clean food. For an historic site to share history in a way that values our visitors as thinking and feeling individuals and not just empty minds waiting to be filled with facts was, I think, truly unexpected.

takeovers encourage visitor participation

Another recent development in the museum field is the cultivation of audience participation which encourages visitors to feel more ownership over what they are learning and more empowerment within the institution. Nina Simon writes in *The Participatory Museum*, "Participatory techniques...are tools that can be used to address particular institutional aspirations to be relevant, multi-vocal, dynamic, responsive, community spaces."[12] Elaine Heumann Gurian sees participation as a means of democratizing public spaces:

12. Nina Simon, *The Participatory Museum* (Santa Cruz CA: Museum 2.0, 2010), 5.

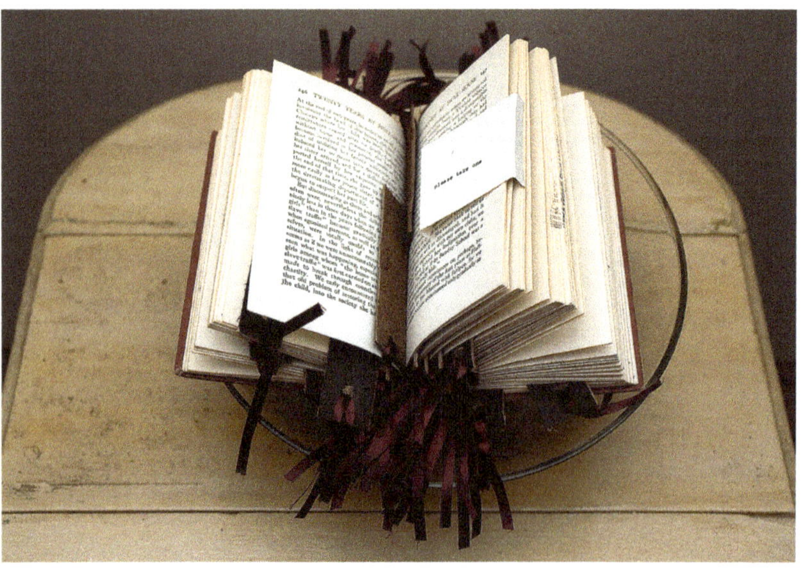

Excavating History Class, *Twenty Years at Hull-House*, 2010

> Museums need to welcome more, share more, and control less. They need to share their space with others—broadening their offerings beyond that which they can provide themselves. And they need to share their collections, their programming, and their content—encouraging others outside the museum staff or invited guests to create, refute, add, and rebut the content associated with the evidence the museum has collected.[13]

In addition to takeovers necessitating the direct participation of artists in museum work, some contemporary art encourages increased visitor participation. The art in *Messing with Jane* was no exception. Many of the visitors' favorite works in the exhibit were participatory. On the simplest level, some pieces invited audiences to take something with them. A sculpture created by the entire class consisted of Addams' autobiography, *Twenty Years at Hull-House*, which was placed open on a glass platter and filled with handmade leather bookmarks displaying "hh" in gold, which stood for Hull-House. Visitors were invited to take these bookmarks home, thereby participating in the handmade revolution and perhaps meditating on the gifts of Hull-House. A riskier yet ultimately successful work was Maral Hashemi's *'from me, to you' (after mrs. stevens).* This sculpture consisted of an antique steamer trunk that was laid open in front of the museum. The tan trunk was filled with spare clothes, shoes, and other objects. The work paid homage to the former head of the Hull-House women's club, whose personal belongings were transferred to a linen trunk upon her death and distributed to her neighbors. Though the trunk bore no label or instructions, it appears that visitors and passersby understood Hashemi's intentions; slowly the materials disappeared throughout the exhibit, with the empty steamer trunk remaining at the exhibit's close.

Erin Obradovich and Allison Jenetopulos created pieces that required more sustained visitor participation. Jenetopulos threaded the front porch of Hull-House and hung keys along the yarn. Each key featured the name of one of the reformers

---

13. Elaine Heumann Gurian, "Museum as Soup Kitchen," *Curator: The Museum Journal* 53:1 (2010), 83.

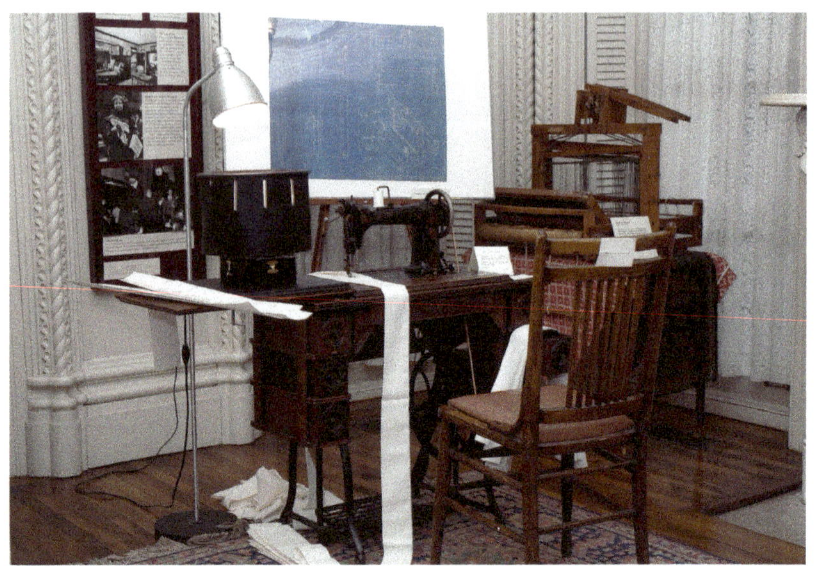

Erin Obradovich, *Sewing Machine Zoetrope*, 2010
interactive installation, altered treadle sewing machine powering a zoetrope, hand drawn animation strips, cloth

who lived and worked at Hull-House, embroidered on a piece of starched white cloth. As visitors entered the museum, they were encouraged to choose a key and therefore identify with one of Hull-House's residents for the remainder of their visit. Upon their exit, visitors were asked to re-hang the key on the string. I was captivated by the idea that visitors might directly identify with a Hull-House resident, and I wonder how artists might further facilitate intimate encounters with historical figures.

Obradovich built a zoetrope, or early animation machine, and displayed it on a push-pedal sewing machine, much like one in the museum's collection. Visitors were encouraged to try using the sewing machine (which spoke volumes about the difficult labor that immigrants in the Hull-House community experienced) and were taught to create drawings that fit within the zoetrope. These simple activities enthralled visitors, taught them about 19th century life, and allowed them to actively participate in the completion of Obradovich's artwork. For JAHHM, this kind of hands-on learning is particularly relevant. Dozens of artists came to live at Hull-House and engage in art creation alongside their immigrant neighbors, and the Settlement's pedagogy was grounded in applied learning. Immigrant neighbors participated in sewing, woodshop, and electric classes at Hull-House as well as in lecture series and literature classes. Obradovich's piece allowed theory to come full circle at Hull-House and has since inspired more embodied forms of learning at the museum. John Dewey, a regular visitor of Addams's and an admirer of Hull-House's educational philosophy, wrote, "I believe that education, therefore, is a process of living and not a preparation for future living."[14]

takeovers require commitment

In many ways, Keller and her class challenged JAHHM to allow the site to be vulnerable in ways the staff hadn't imagined. This too is a central aspect of takeovers. After all, sharing power and knowledge doesn't come easily to institutions or individuals. As we collaborated, it became clear that, like Fred Wilson, some students would want to use artifacts in the museum's collection, taking them beyond the Plexiglas case and moving the exhibit beyond the walls of the museum. In the end, this project required a real commitment, at all institutional levels, to be successful.

It didn't take long for JAHHM staff to recognize that it was risky and time-intensive to facilitate the use of artifacts in our collection. Hannah Merry asked to borrow some historic neighborhood paving blocks from our collection. In a meditative performance called *Journey to the Hull-House*, Merry planned to carry a suitcase full of the blocks from the former site of Chicago's train station to the front steps of Hull-House. The blocks would then be integrated into a site-specific sculpture and documentation of the performance. The museum staff deliberated on whether and how Merry could use the blocks. Certainly the paving blocks were sturdy (each one weighed over 20 pounds) and would not be damaged by this use. The collection contains at least a hundred of these blocks, so they aren't unique objects. But would a loan form be needed? What about insurance, since the stones would be taken off the premises? Ultimately, Merry was not able to use

14. John Dewey, *School Journal* 54 (January 1897) 77-80.

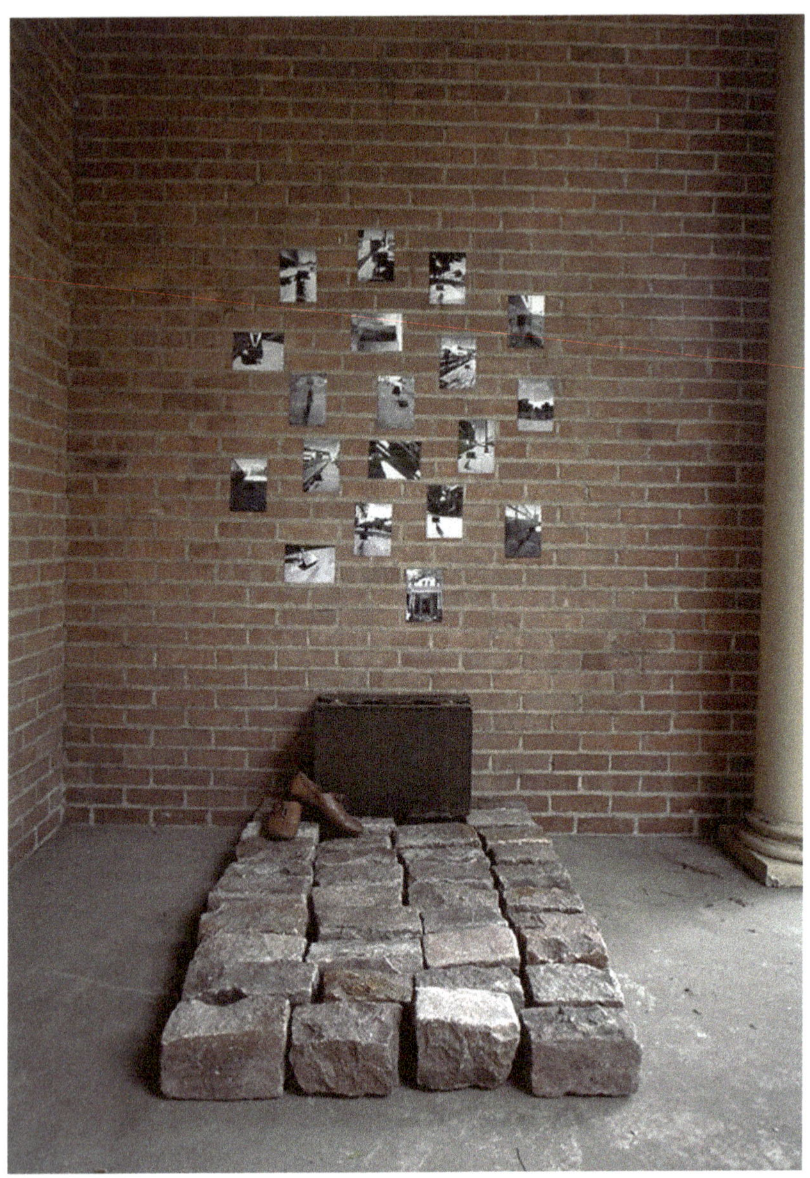

Hannah Merry, *Journey*, 2010
performance and installation: bricks, original paving stones from Halsted Street, vintage suitcase, photos, worn shoes, 7 x 5 x 4 feet
Merry filled a a suitcase with bricks and dragged it from the site of the former train station, where immigrants arrived during Addams's time, the two miles to Hull House, re-enacting their exhausting and dangerous journey. For a time, so many young women immigrants were preyed upon that Addams started sending people to meet trains in case anyone needed her help.

the historic bricks in her performance, but they were used for the on-site sculpture. Curatorial associate Teresa Silva reflected on these challenges after the exhibit closed: "In the future, participants should be aware that, if borrowing artifacts from the Museum, there are some conditions that need to be considered before the item is allocated (in the case of a loan, proof of insurance is necessary)." Clearly the artist-students were charting new territory and engaging central questions about the role of museums when it comes to the access and the preservation of artifacts.

Thankfully, the class understood that these were new questions for the museum, and to me the partnership felt like a true collaboration. We worked through the issues together, often with enthusiasm. Keller's own piece required the most dialog before it could be installed. As a reference to Hull-House's history of ceramics, she covered one room of the museum with terra cotta colored clay, supported by a cardboard backing. The oil-based clay would remain soft, to continue the Hull House history of allowing people to "leave their mark." This was a true challenge for Michael Plummer, the museum's historic preservationist, who is charged with maintaining the facilities. Drilling into the walls was not an option, but the panels were so heavy that hanging them would be difficult. Ultimately Plummer and Keller arrived at a solution together, but this would not have happened without the museum staff's full participation and desire for the museum to be used in new ways. Plummer reflected,

> I generally love the idea of collaboration with others—artists, educators, historians, etc. It's triple-beneficial. We allow our space to be used as inspiration for those coming in to collaborate, we then see our space in a new light, and museum visitors are treated to a richer, more vibrant and nuanced experience. I thought all of the SAIC projects worked toward this goal. I appreciated the SAIC group's willingness to respect the historic character and fabric of the space and develop appropriate installations.

There were still others who needed to be on board with the project. Our museum educators themselves had to learn about the pieces since they worked on the front lines to help visitors interpret and engage with the exhibit. Officials on campus of the University of Illinois at Chicago, where JAHHM is located, had to be tolerant of our outdoor pieces, which was ultimately our biggest challenge. The museum staff understood the exhibit and its untraditional components but the campus facilities professionals, it turned out, did not. Site-specific installations by Cori Williams and Liene Bosquê, which had served to pique the curiosity of passers-by and draw attention to the exhibit, became a problem when the university needed to mow our grounds. Ultimately I had to remove elements of Bosquê's piece myself at the close of the exhibition in order to allow the grounds people to do their job.

One of my favorite pieces fared worse. Chiara Galimberti made life-sized canvas silhouettes of 19th century immigrants and embroidered them with provocative quotations from contemporary immigrants. These pieces were attached to the exterior walls of the museum, the fence surrounding Hull-House, and surrounding light posts. I had spoken to the adjacent campus center's director about the project, but within 24 hours, the silhouettes were removed from the fence and light posts by another unit. Despite persistent calls, no one responded to tell me who moved the pieces or where they could be found. It was an utter disappointment. Galimberti could not have worked with the university on this matter; it was my responsibility to act as a liaison, but I hadn't anticipated such a strong reaction.

the future of takeovers

The process of creating the *Messing with Jane* exhibit demonstrated to the JAHHM staff that contemporary art is not at odds with an historic house museum, that in fact, they make for wonderful partners. At this time, JAHHM has plans to host a contemporary art biennial, a project that came directly out of our collaboration with the Excavating History class. Emerging and professional artists will be asked to reflect on the history and spirit of Hull-House and create installations and relational art in our space and elsewhere around the city. K-12 students will engage in art making as well, bringing new voices and perspectives to the museum. JAHHM has also launched an Alternative Labeling Project where we present audiences with multiple narratives to demonstrate the complexities of history. For 2011,

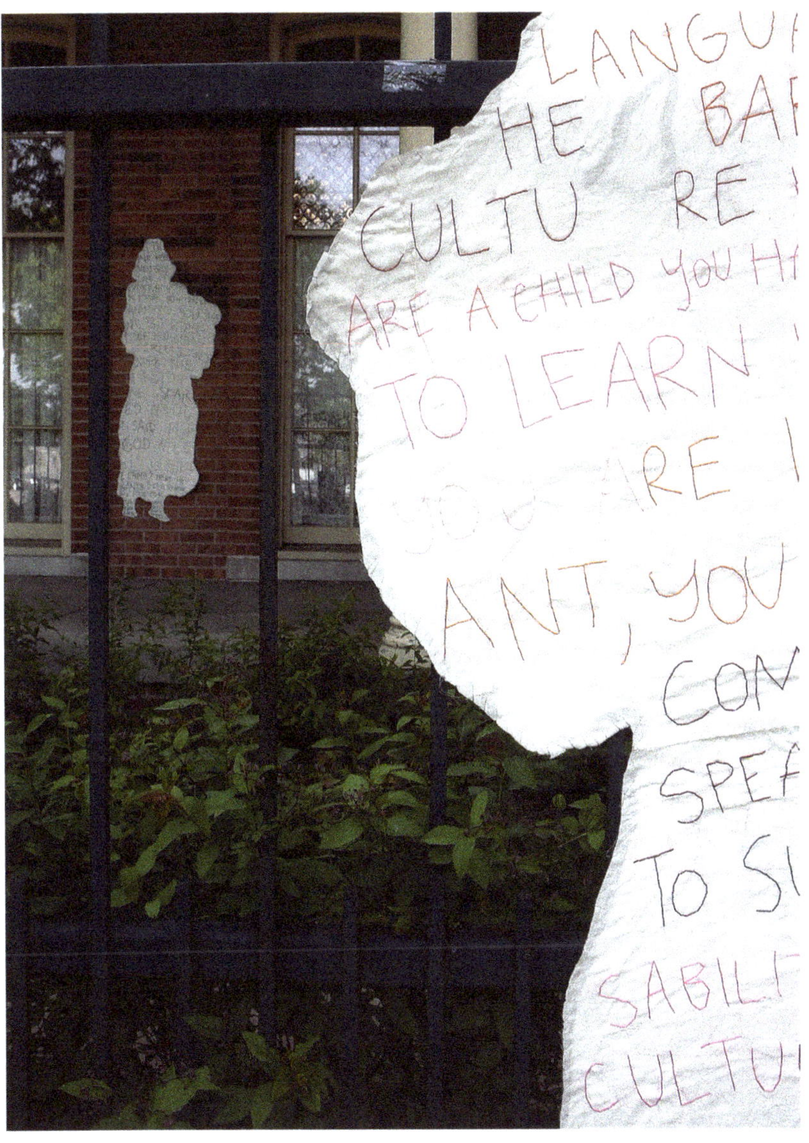

Chiara Galimberti, *Present Pasts*, 2010
photo Emerson Granillo

we have asked a contemporary music ensemble, a poet, and a performance artist to interpret objects from our collection and create museum labels in their medium.

I see the *Messing with Jane* exhibit as the first expression of an artistic coup within an historic house museum. The takeover is a first step in changing the nature of museums: of history and how we tell it, of what we value, and of who gets to choose. But there are more opportunities for museums to allow for the unexpected, the unconventional, and the unspoken, to allow their visitors and other members of the public to intervene and help shape historic sites. Clearly this work requires that museums give up control and invite some messiness into their work. But there is much to be gained as well. Historic house museums have much to offer, but their gifts are best excavated collectively, with curators and educators and artists and visitors. Viva la Revolución!

right: visitors participating in Erin Obradovich's *Sewing Machine Zoetrope*

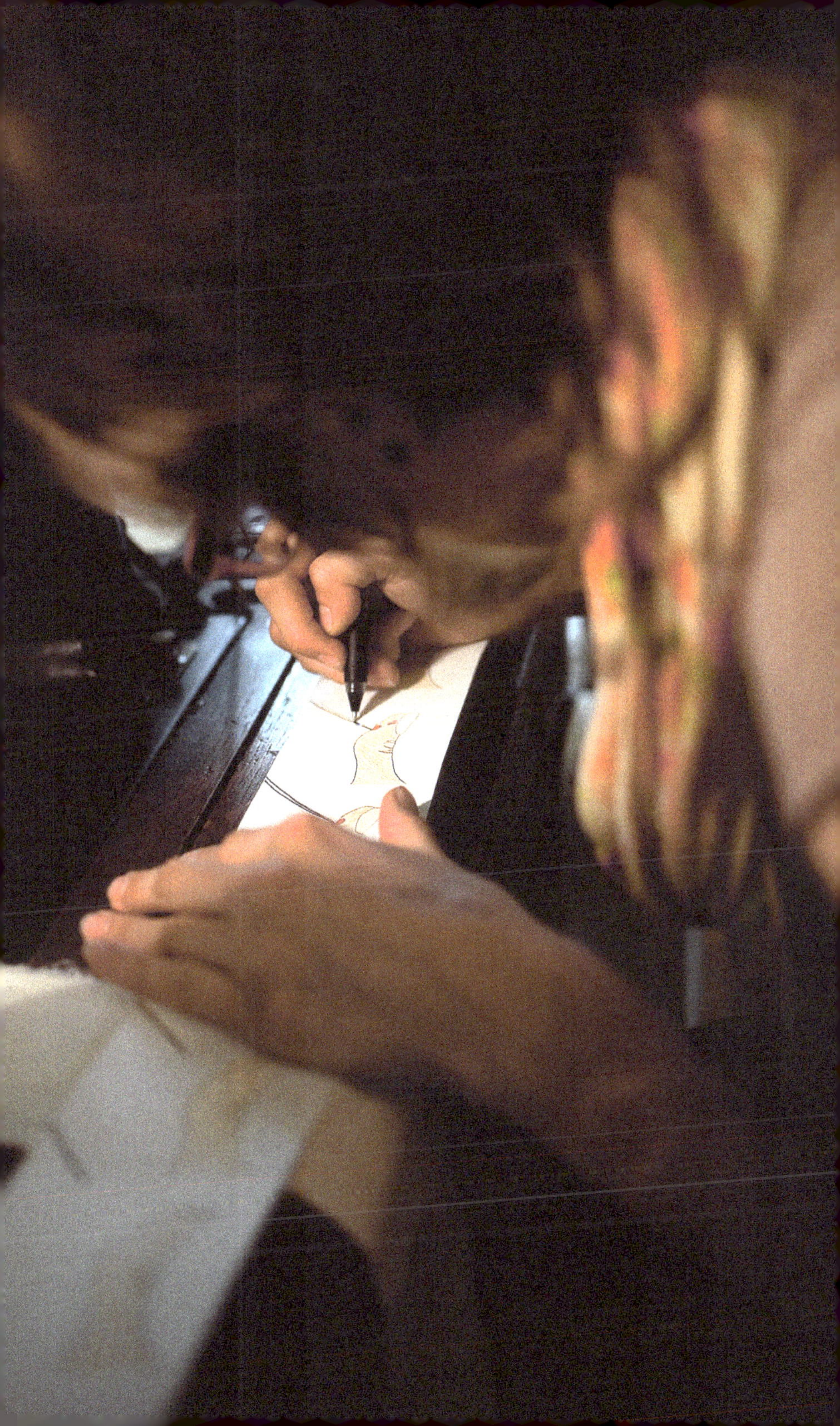

What
puns,
what
replacing

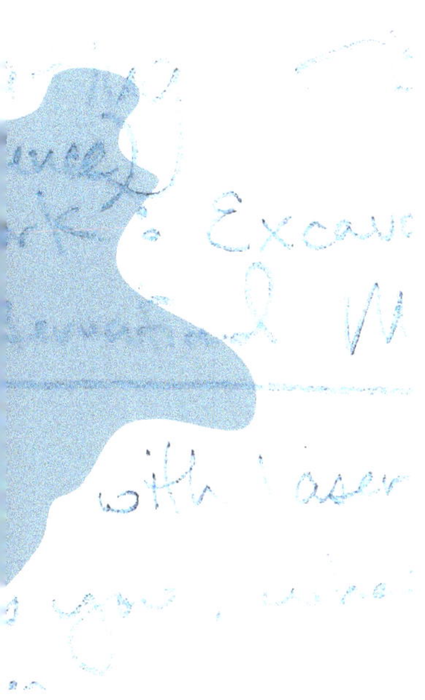

a proliferation of metaphors, and art-making like baseball

rebecca keller

Deciding on a specific image to refer to any complex endeavor (say, for example, the cover of this book) reveals just how many metaphors are in operation in the world and how once-sturdy paradigms can no longer reflect the evolution of one's experience or work.

{**metaphor:** *a figure of speech that uses an image, a story or a thing to represent some quality or idea. i.e.: "The artist in her studio is like a scientist in her lab." Or, "The exhibitions in a museum are like an archive of decision-making." More broadly, metaphor may also be used to describe any figure of speech that relies on association, comparison, or resemblance. In this broader sense, antithesis ("History is a set of* *dry facts, set in stone...”), metonymy (“The word “history” standing in for a set of broadly defined practices, ideas, and sets of information.”) and simile (“The artist is like an excavator.”) can all be considered types of metaphor.*}

{**paradigm:** *The model we carry around in our heads—a theoretical framework or pattern of thought (“The place an artist works is called a studio.” or, “An artwork is a discreet object with a separate and distinct identity, an inherent ontological wholeness.”)*}

Post-studio is an increasingly common term referring to an altered paradigm that replaces the image of the artist in her studio with the image of the artist working in a variety of ways and places: in a studio, yes, but also on her computer in a coffee shop; or creating a participatory artwork with passersby in a park; or meeting with local archivists on a research project. Thinking about “studio” as a place gives way to the notion of “studio as time”: time spent creatively engaging, researching, and discussing, as well as making.

The artist is researcher
maker
collaborator
curator
organizer
storyteller
narrator

As a practice, *Excavating History* is elastic and multifaceted, and the boundaries fencing it off from other aspects of my creative life are blurry. It is an expanding and contracting process and structure that may adopt the characteristics of a class, a collaborative workshop, or an exhibition. It is simultaneously an individual artistic practice, a publishing project, and an ad-hoc collective.

So here’s another for the list: the artist as boundary-blurrer.

One outcome of the collaborative nature of these projects is that there is now a growing family of people—artists, educators, museum directors, historians, preservationists—who have become invested in the work.

I am happy to note that we have left a trace in the world.

The Jane Addams Hull-House Museum has gone on to develop other projects with artists—a move the staff and director attribute to their experience with *Excavating History.* The City of Chicago gave Briana Schweizer the go-ahead to pursue a public project she initially developed in the Cultural Center/ *Excavating History* residency, which she was able to realize during "Taste of Chicago," one of the city's most popular public events. And many people beyond the art- or historic-site audience benefited from the Red Cross blood drive and the Working Bikes bicycle collection that took place as part of the Pleasant Home exhibition. Add to the list: the artist as meaning-generator. As change-maker.

Some of my former students are now artists with highly developed professional practices ranging from studio-based work to collaborations to performance. Others have moved more deeply into research. Regardless of their particular practice, many have expressed the desire to work together again—which brings me to the International Museum of Surgical Science, and the baseball metaphor.

In spring 2011, I met with Lindsey Thieman, the curator of the International Museum of Surgical Science, to discuss the possibility of an exhibition during Chicago Artists Month. The resulting exhibition and residency, *Body of Work: Excavating History at the International Museum of Surgical Science,* involved the coming together of an ad hoc collective comprised of former students, colleagues, scientists and other collaborators.

skype, email, and faith

The organizing process for the exhibition was, shall we say, challenging. It involved sharing research and images as well as developing concepts and space considerations among twelve

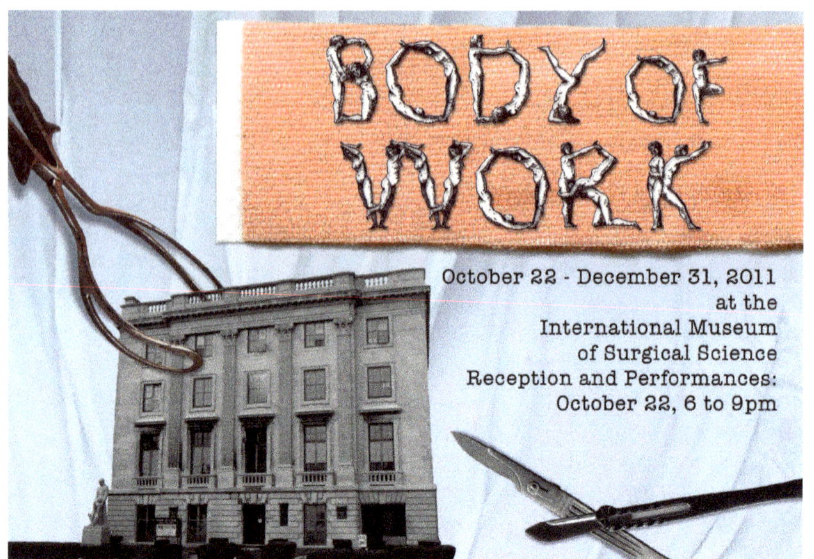

Body of Work postcard, International Museum of Surgical Science, 2011, design by Briana Schweizer

very busy people, at least several of whom, at any given time, were in another state, country, or time zone. In the beginning, we met at the museum to get acquainted with the collections and the staff, to share ideas, and to flesh out our expectations. But as schedules became more and more difficult to coordinate and as travel dates loomed, we turned to other means. Elise Goldstein organized a wiki-space for us, a digi-puddle where we shared files, information, interests and links. Rebecca Hernandez posted a documentary on a Victorian pharmacy. Lindsey Thieman and Jack Whalen of the IMSS were enormously responsive in finding resources and archives. We exchanged photos and documents and YouTube videos and books. For those whose schedules precluded more time in the museum, we posted photos and video walk-throughs. Anyone heading to the museum would send out an email, and many impromptu research meetings resulted.

A revolving assembly of the collective met weekly via Skype. It was always fun to see what the tech issue of the evening would be. Distracting echoes? People able to hear only some others, and those people not able to hear each other? Dropped connections? Sometimes a traveling member was able to secure an Internet connection only in a public café, and so would listen on headphones and type comments or questions in a chat window. At one point Joe Cruz, unable to get online, participated by phoning Rebecca Hernandez, who held her cell phone near the computer speaker so Joe could hear the conversation, and then gave Rebecca his comments, which she relayed. I love that example, because it illustrates how, with a little good faith, a willingness to help one another, and a desire to privilege communication over any (imagined) perfect technological fix, we somehow managed to put together a workable system.

I shared numerous conversations with each artist about the conceptual development and plans for the work. However, as the date of the opening approached I have to admit that, as the organizer, I did wish for a better sense of what the finished works would actually look like and how they would sit in the space. Then I would remind myself how intelligent and inventive these artists are. Keep the faith.

artmaking like baseball: running the bases

There are differences between a group exhibition and a collective. In a group show, a curator decides on the theme and chooses artworks or invites artists whose works have a particular relationship to that theme. The curator may decide to tease out similarities or differences of approach via juxtaposition or by discussing them in certain terms. Conversely, in many collectives, all the work is jointly created and the authorship shared.

But the Excavating History collective in *Body of Work* differed from each of these models. Even though we functioned as a collective, each of us was also able to pursue individual artworks. In the end it was like a baseball team. Each of us created and exhibited our own work (analogous to a time "at bat," or the opportunity to make the important catch). But each of us was deeply committed to the collective effort—all of us were invested in making the entire exhibition—and everyone participating in it—look good. One person's big catch or well-hit ball benefited all of us.

This collectivity was manifested in a variety of ways. Perhaps the most obvious was the shared work of getting an exhibition mounted: designing labels, editing copy, picking up supplies, sharing materials and physical assistance, offering to put up out-of-town artists, giving people rides, bringing potluck contributions during installation. But what was most extraordinary were the discussions and critical feedback we offered one another. Skype sessions, meetings at the museum, phone conversations, and coffee dates became opportunities for airing conceptual directions, running through possibilities, solving problems, and brainstorming. Ideas and connections emerged in conversation that would not have occurred to each of us individually. Ways to solve vexing technical or installation issues were explored. Esoteric pathways of research that one of us stumbled upon became central and generative to another. There was an uncanny sense of things working out: spaces that more than one person wanted to respond to somehow accommodated the work; a problem with installing an artwork in a fragile space got solved.

This process led, inevitably, to the artworks' being in richer conversation with one another, and with the collections and the site than if we had all worked in isolation and simply arrived on install day, carrying our supplies and individual toolkits. The process both informed our work and enlarged our capabilities. The combined creativity, skill and imagination of the group added to the resources we each could draw upon in making our individual artworks. It enabled all of us, (to extend the metaphor) to swing for the fences.

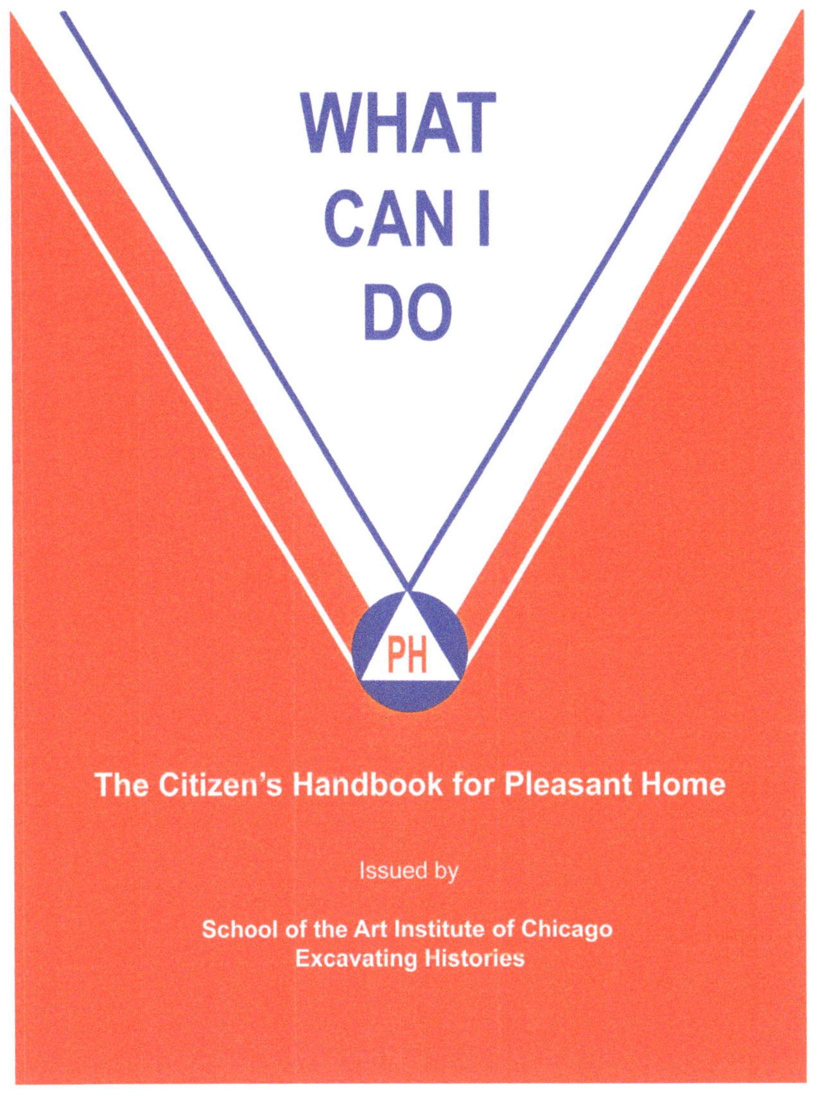

Pleasant Home Victory Pamphlet, 2008
pamphlet designed by Amber Ginsburg, edited by Rebecca Keller

following spread: Natalie Pfister, *Ware/Where/Wear, an installation in porcelain*, 2008, Pleasant Home

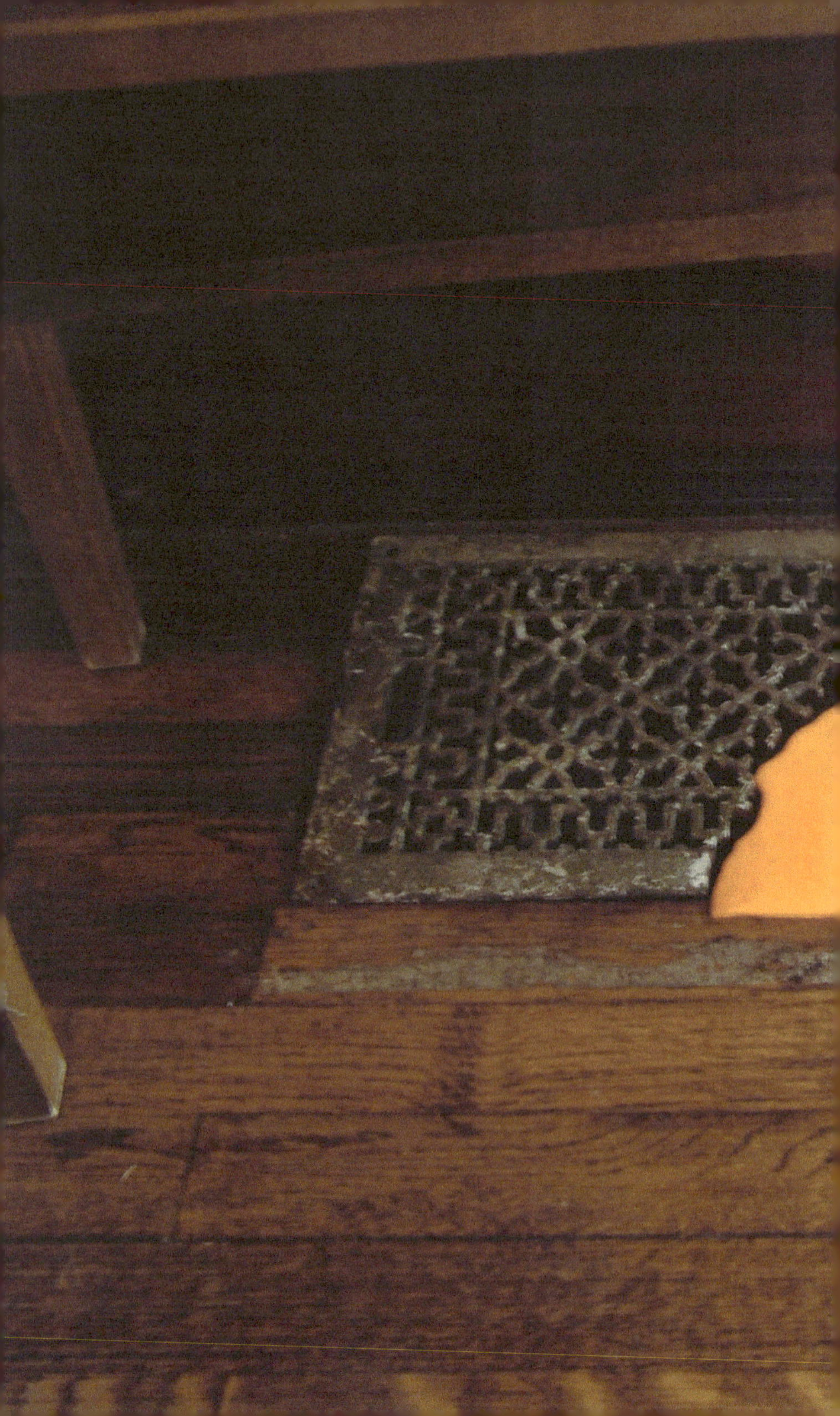

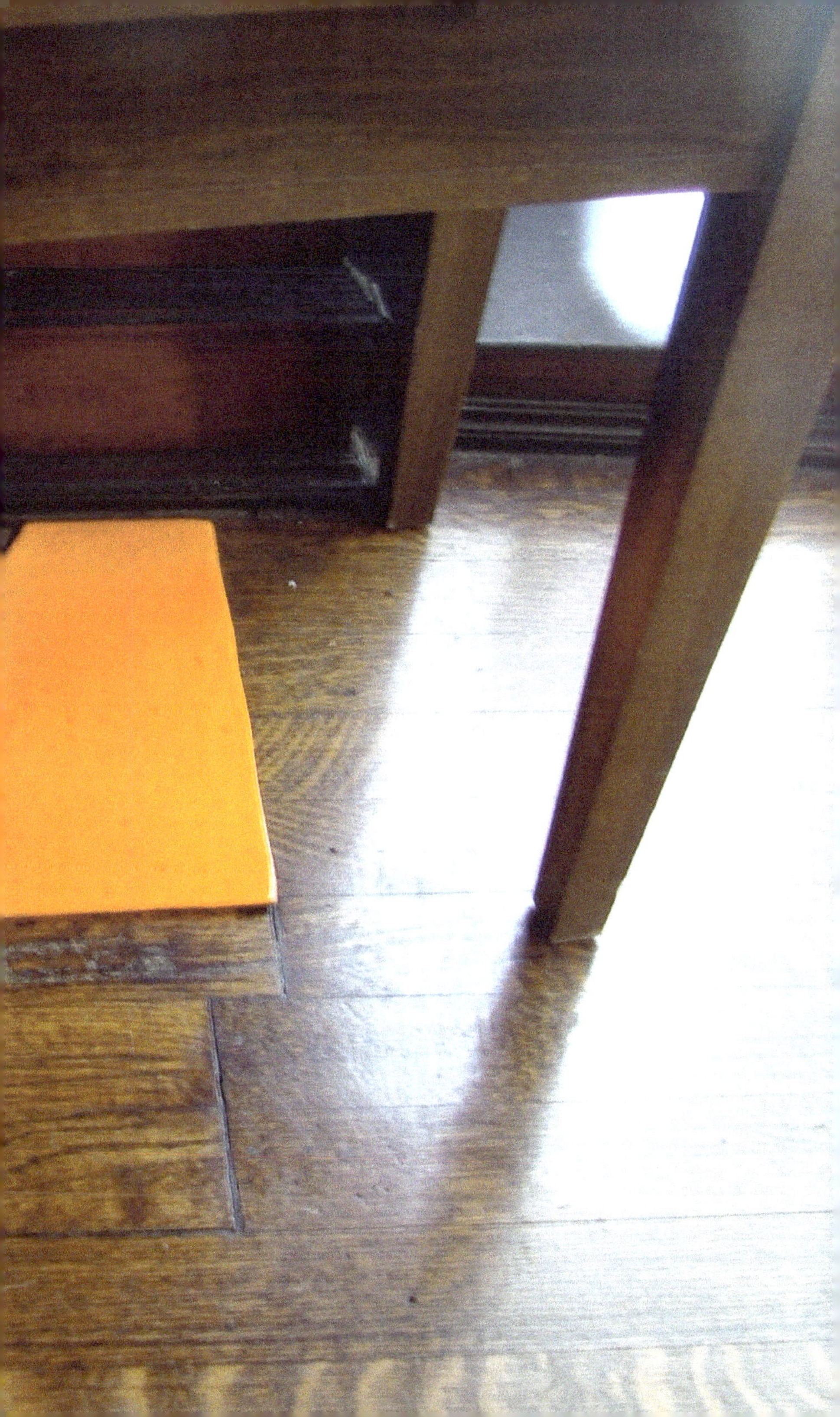

...e deadlines to be g...

c. 7 | images of ...
or sketches...

print delivery
deadline

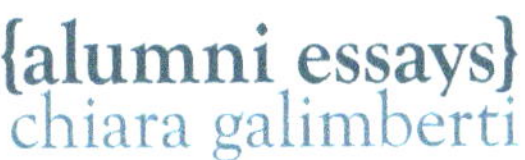

What are you doing now that still reflects the interests/methodologies/conceptual frameworks related to Excavating History?

CG: I was just accepted to the GFRY studio, which is a collaborative effort bringing together students from all disciplines to work towards innovative and socially grounded projects. This year we are designing sustainable disaster relief in Chile in collaboration with Chilean designers and organizers. The Excavating Histories Project I was involved with worked with the Hull-House in Chicago, which provided an incredible source of inspiration for the possibilities held by combining creative thinking and social justice issues.

What were the challenges of the project? How were you able to allow for your own interests and predilections while working within the framework of the site and project?

CG: Being part of Excavating Histories was an incredible effort in collaboration stemming from listening instead of imposing. Rebecca made sure we knew each other as people and fostered a sense of communal effort. On one of the first days of class, she had us talk to each other about ourselves and build trust. It was an unprecedented approach to learning, one that is more holistic, and thus avoids many of the trappings of traditional academia, be it unhealthy competition or unbalanced class dynamics.

How were you able to import your own pre-existing aesthetic interests and conditions into the process and out of it again (vis a vis the dominant sort of white cube training and exhibition possibilities)?

CG: For starters, there was never any imposition on how we as students were supposed to conceive our input in the project. Rebecca never told us that we could not use the space as a gallery in a more traditional sense, or that we had to privilege one mode of communication at the expense of another. Instead she listened and tried to provide whatever tools we needed to bring our ideas to fruition.

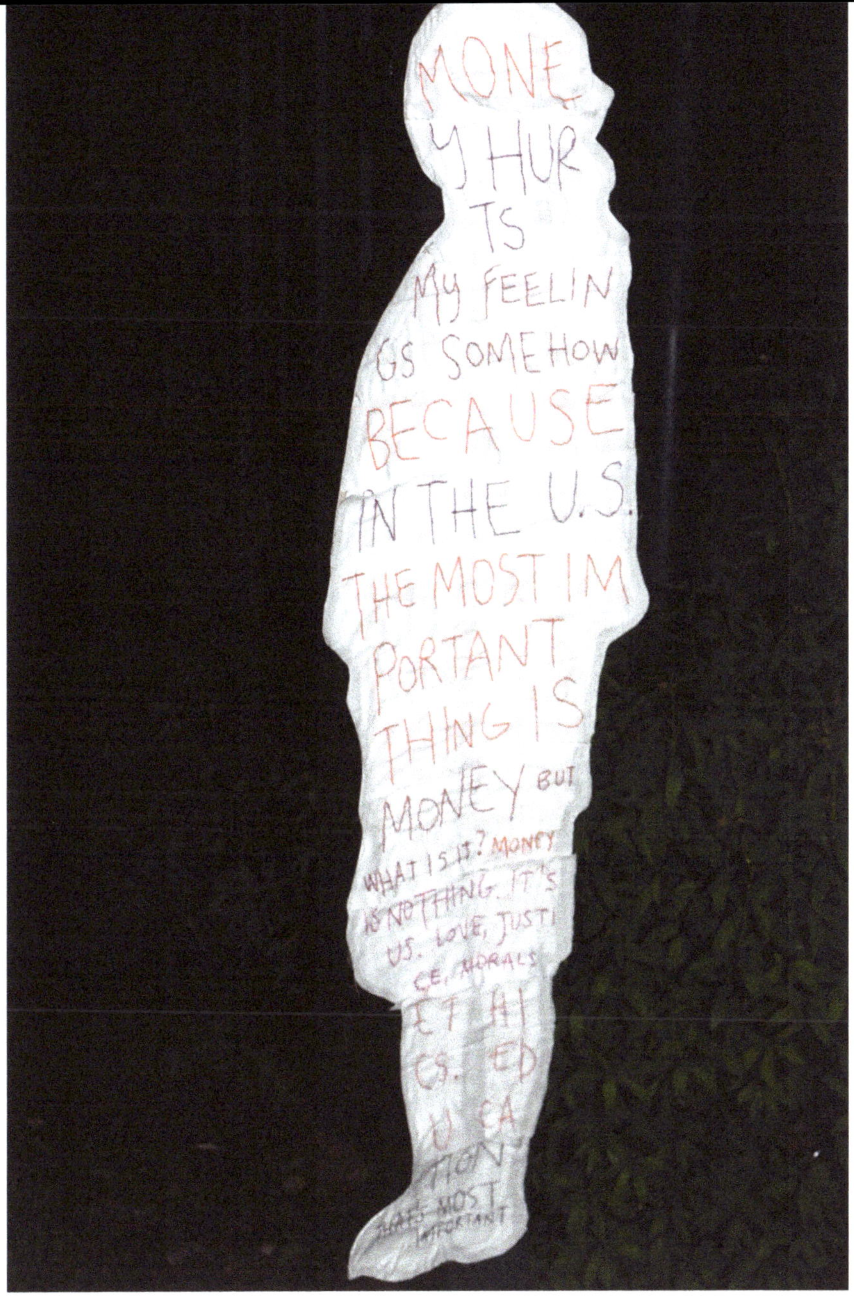

Chiara Galimberti, *Present Pasts*, 2010
photo Emerson Granillo

· medicalization of food

e / Remain

Going off your meds
slip someone a Micky
hide it under your tongue
pill heads
pill popper
blue beanies "Yellow Submarine"
"we're not candy" public service
pill BOX (hats)

{alumni essays}

elise goldstein

Throughout my life, I have been taught that history is a dusty, static thing. It has been decidedly resolved. The events which have passed are sealed, immovable and buried, much like their enactors. The remaining contents of history must be handled in moisture-regulated rooms with white gloves and pent-in breath, a scene which turns a sneeze into an earthquake, and a splinter into a relic. This approach is accompanied by a consistent sentiment, "You cannot change history, but you can choose to learn from it." Very rarely have I heard such an unsatisfying declaration. But history is full of declarations.

Behind each declaration is an assumption.
If History is recorded and resolved, then we assume:
No one keeps secrets.

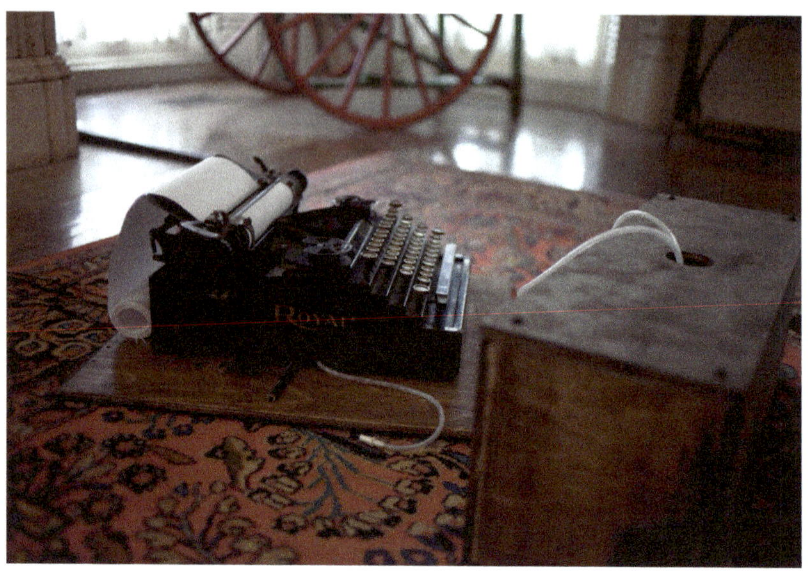

Elise Goldstein, *The Ink Well* (detail), 2010
installation view in the parlor of the Hull-House Museum
photo Emerson Granillo

Everyone tells the truth.
Language is objective.
The authorities are always right.
People are best judged by their observed actions, only.

The tidiness of history turns living, suffering, striving, complex, fallible, conflicted people into characters of bedtime stories. History, if observed in this way, is essentially dehumanizing.

Excavating History complicates.

That act of complication acknowledges the subtleties of the past, unearths the nature of previously lived experience, and transforms the perceived stasis of history into a breathing, responsive organism.

Excavating History is a methodology through which I have been compelled to question the punctuation of history: the period.

I must attempt to continue through the grammar of inquiry. I must strive not to declare, but rather to *ask*.

What is the difference between History and the Past?
What is the language of preservation?
What can an archive reveal of one's personhood?
What is worth saving?

How does one democratize the narrative of History?
How, as artists, can we offer voice? Whose voice?
How can I best remind myself of the infinite potential in remembrance and response?
How can the past be observed and absorbed by something beyond the intellect?

Am I able to resist the urge to believe that these questions can definitively be answered?
Am I able to resist the desire to resolve the past?

...rray M. Kwan M.D)

[illegible] pic For M. H. Kwan [illegible]

A [illegible]

[illegible]

D negative [illegible]

d [illegible] [illegible]

a [illegible] giving [illegible]

[illegible] [illegible]

something [illegible]

myself [illegible] Don't know what

to do, can't say [illegible]

[illegible].

blood drawing

thread from [illegible]

probably from [illegible]

is Korea, not China. [illegible]

D, not A

merchants visited "Gorgeo" in

[illegible] 13th century (look-up)

[illegible] thread (with blood) "The

{alumni essay}
briana schweizer

it's about time

It is impossible to understand the present without knowing the past, yet we often assume things about the world around us without really knowing how we got here. In the practice of Excavating History, particularities are explored and (re)presented with the intent of expanding specificity. This practice adds layers and impressions to places we pass by or inhabit, that we think we know, in order to know them better.

Typically, my practice is devoted to investigating and responding to historical moments found in public spaces. In creating my own versions of "monuments" to celebrate the (conventionally) anti-monumental, my *Monuments to the Unmomentous* series speaks the language of monuments

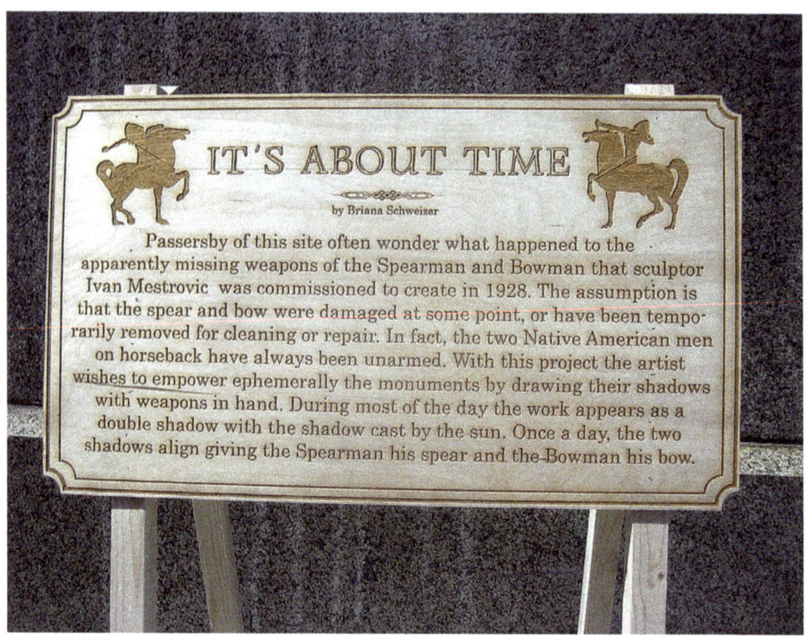

Briana Schweizer, *It's About Time*, 2009
outdoor drawing, charcoal, wood, 25 x 15 feet

and seeks to reclaim public space to include the disenfranchised. While I relied on research about the topics I was working with, these pieces did not reference specific past moments. The *It's About Time* project added the challenge of speaking directly to a historical event. What is the process of discovery? How does that process influence what one finds? What version of history do you choose to believe? And, what remains hidden?

I developed *It's About Time* while working with Rebecca Keller and the students of Excavating History. I became interested in a particular pair of monuments on Michigan Avenue and Congress Parkway. *The Spearman* and *The Bowman* by Ivan Mestrovic attracted me because the two Native Americans represented appear in the decisive moment of using their respective weapons. Yet the weapons themselves are noticeably missing. At first I thought they must have been stolen, or perhaps had been temporarily removed for cleaning or preservation. When I asked people who had lived in Chicago for a long time, many distinctly recalled seeing them there at some point; some even had stories for why they weren't there any longer. However, a bit of research turned up the fact that they had never existed. In fact, the artist explains that he left them out in order to intensify the expectation of the moment, and that the sculpture was a tribute to and celebration of Native American contributions to Chicago and the nation. Seen through a contemporary lens, this doesn't seem right. Instead, they communicate a disarmament, making them vulnerable and powerless—telling the story of Native culture overwhelmed by new American power while simultaneously exoticizing and eroticizing the warriors and wrapping Manifest Destiny in nostalgia. This monument, fraught with contradiction, was irresistible as a subject. Through the Excavating History class residency at the Cultural Center, I met Nathan Mason, curator of public art in Chicago, who invited me to make a temporary intervention on the monument to coincide with an annual Chicago festival.

With a team of eight people, we traced the monuments' shadows in a couple of minutes. We spent the next two days filling in the tracing with a light grey "shadow" drawing and adding the "missing" weapons to those images. A pair of signs explained the project to passersby. My drawings slowly faded away with weather over the course of the next few months, but each day for a moment in time the real shadows were aligned with the drawings, "arming" and empowering the monuments.

Collection of data doesn't automatically increase our knowledge of a situation. In the context of Excavating History, it is the artist's job to perform the alchemy to add understanding to data. However, we must assume that we are as affected by our point of view as are our subjects. There will be contemporary sentiments about which we will be perceived as wrong-headed in the future. Similarly, we are likely to have faulty assumptions about the past from our vantage in the present. I feel that my interpretation of *The Spearman* and *The Bowman*, reached by careful process, research, and consideration for ideas in the present and past, is important and "correct." However, Mestrovic believed he was celebrating Native

Americans with his creation. We have the ability and right to reevaluate past beliefs. The only way we will continue to know history is through constant questioning and reevaluation. History is ever changing, and to tackle it one must accept the likelihood that one day our histories will be revisited by those in the then-present future.

right: Briana Schweizer, *It's About Time*, 2009

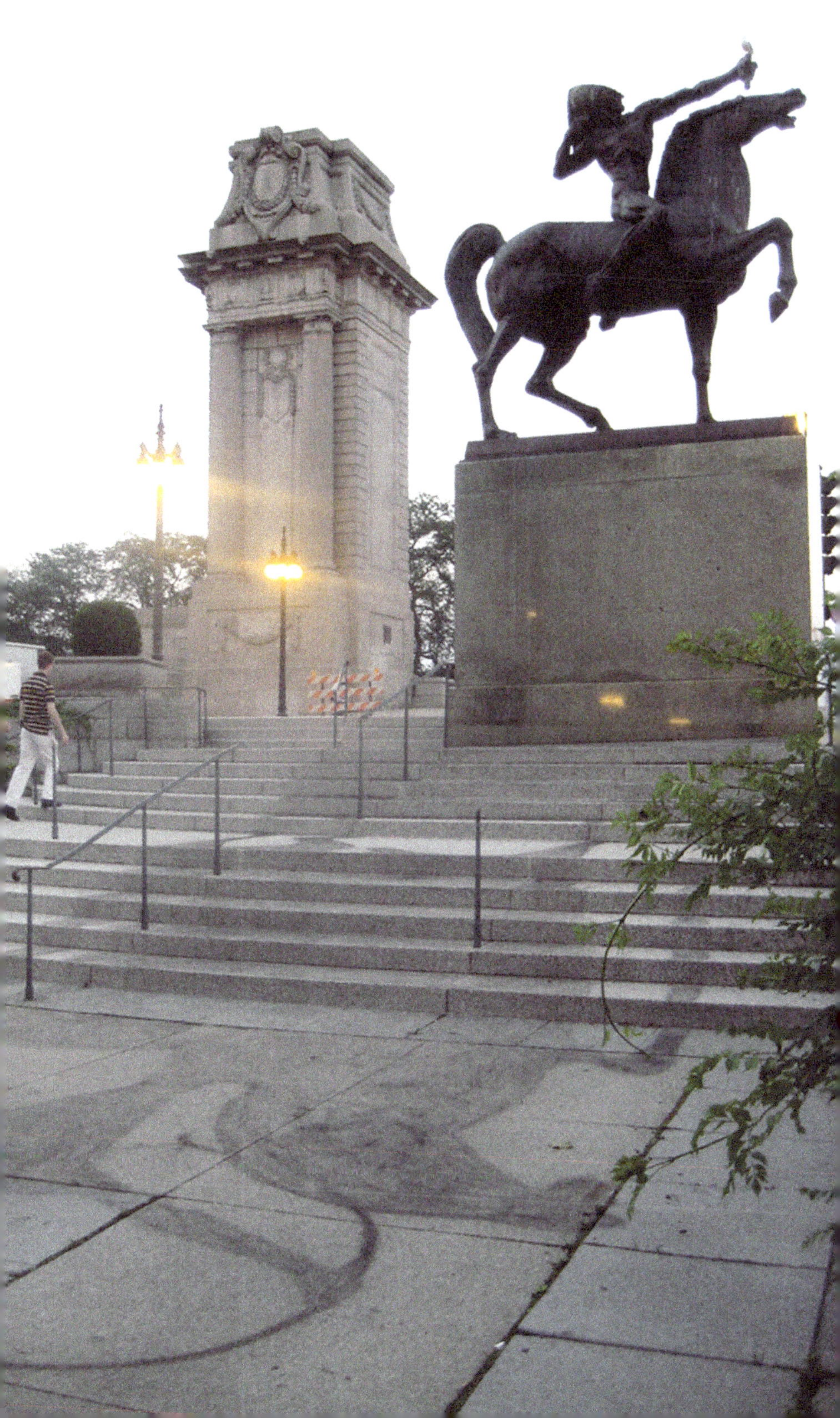

Hard Cand

3 3/4 cups

1 1/2 cups

1 cup wat

flavoring

hancements

To do:

finish, print & roll h

wrap candies

~~[illegible]~~

~~[illegible]~~

future assignme

fall contacts

sign for candie

sign for guid

{alumni essay}
amber ginsburg

As a graduate student, Excavating History appealed because the course description mirrored, practically verbatim, my artist statement and reflected my practice. There was such synergy between Rebecca's approach to history and mine that I took the course twice. I was interested in using history as a tool to comment on the present by looking backwards. But Rebecca's remarkable ability to draw out the interests and diverse talents of each student opened up history as a tool allowing, among other things, playfulness and fantasy within historical narratives. Over the last few years, there has been a slow evolution in my work, which I attribute to the experience of collectively developing an exhibition with such a multiplicity of approaches to history.

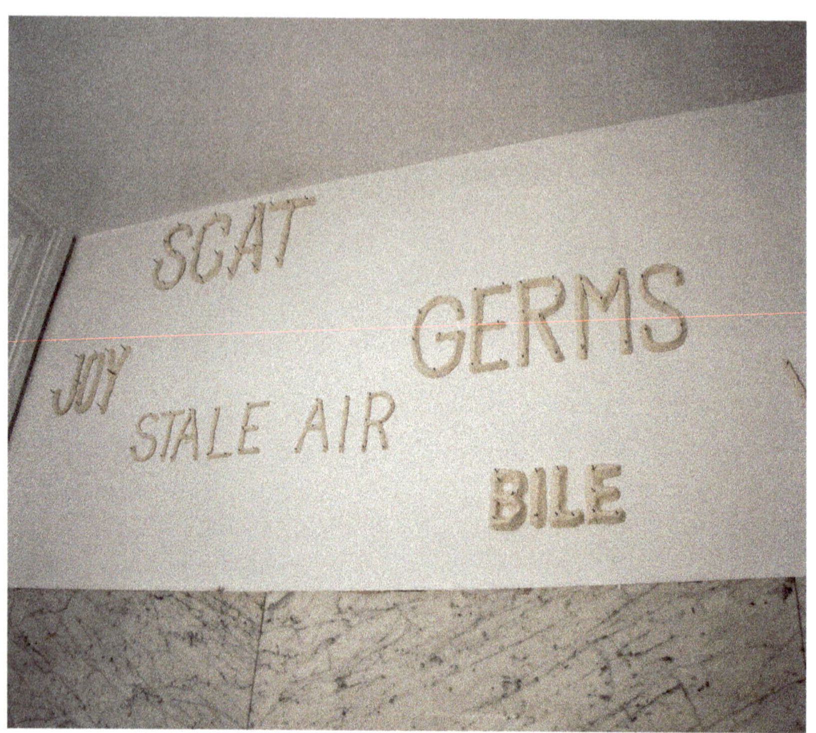

Amber Ginsburg, *Knob* (detail), 2011
porcelain, installed in the bathrooms at the International Museum of Surgical Science in Chicago
photo Annie Heckman

In both courses, my projects plucked little-known narratives/facts from the past and re-inserted them into the present. In the empty Pleasant Home kitchen, I used the olfactory as a mnemonic device; I populated the shelves with a set of dishes made out of cinnamon. The dishes elicited a response to congregate and recall. I was interested in the kitchen as a site of transition between the public and private and the family and their servants. In a historic home completed in 1897, the relationship between domestic and the domestics has a parallel in the relationship between the expansion of the spice trade (fueled by the desire for cinnamon) and the entrenchment of colonial power structures. A prompt to this parallel was instigated through text, while an enactment of a long history of stories being told in the kitchen happens spontaneously. This project is an exemplar of strategies I applied to other Excavating

History projects, in which present actions evoked past events. Whether I was making victory garden "seed bombs," or noting geographic time with a line demarcating a watershed rendered obsolete by the re-engineered Chicago River, or walking the length of a plat map chain (the tool that made the western United States a tidy grid)—all of my projects employed a timeline that had a dot at now and an arrow pointing backwards.

Research and history are still the initiating force of my practice but something quite unexpected has entered the work. In the past year, I have been thinking about history, not as a revelatory tool, but as a point of imagination. Rather striving to bring the past to the present, I have begun to consider the present as a midpoint and imaging an equally distant future. In doing so, the past becomes a poetic springboard.

For *Past Present Perfect*, a recent exhibition in Iowa City, I invented part of speech to accompany a project, based on an imagined future. Thinking of the gallery as a museum of the not-yet-happened, the works were investigations or encounters with fragments of dishware based on a possible future when we have forgotten what to do with them.

Having been so rooted in revealing a-heroic and little known histories, this 180 degree rotation on the timeline towards the future comes as a surprise. There was something fearless in Rebecca's approach to bringing fifteen diverse minds to a project based on a specific history. No idea was too outlandish or tangential to be explored and teased out. The class functioned as a collective brainstorm and workshop. All that collective teasing-out unhinged me from a clear working path of thinking about the past to thinking about the future.

following spread: Briana Schweizer, *Take Me, I am the Drug, Take Me, I am Hallucinogenic*, 2011, laser-cut paper, paint, glass
photo Rebecca Keller

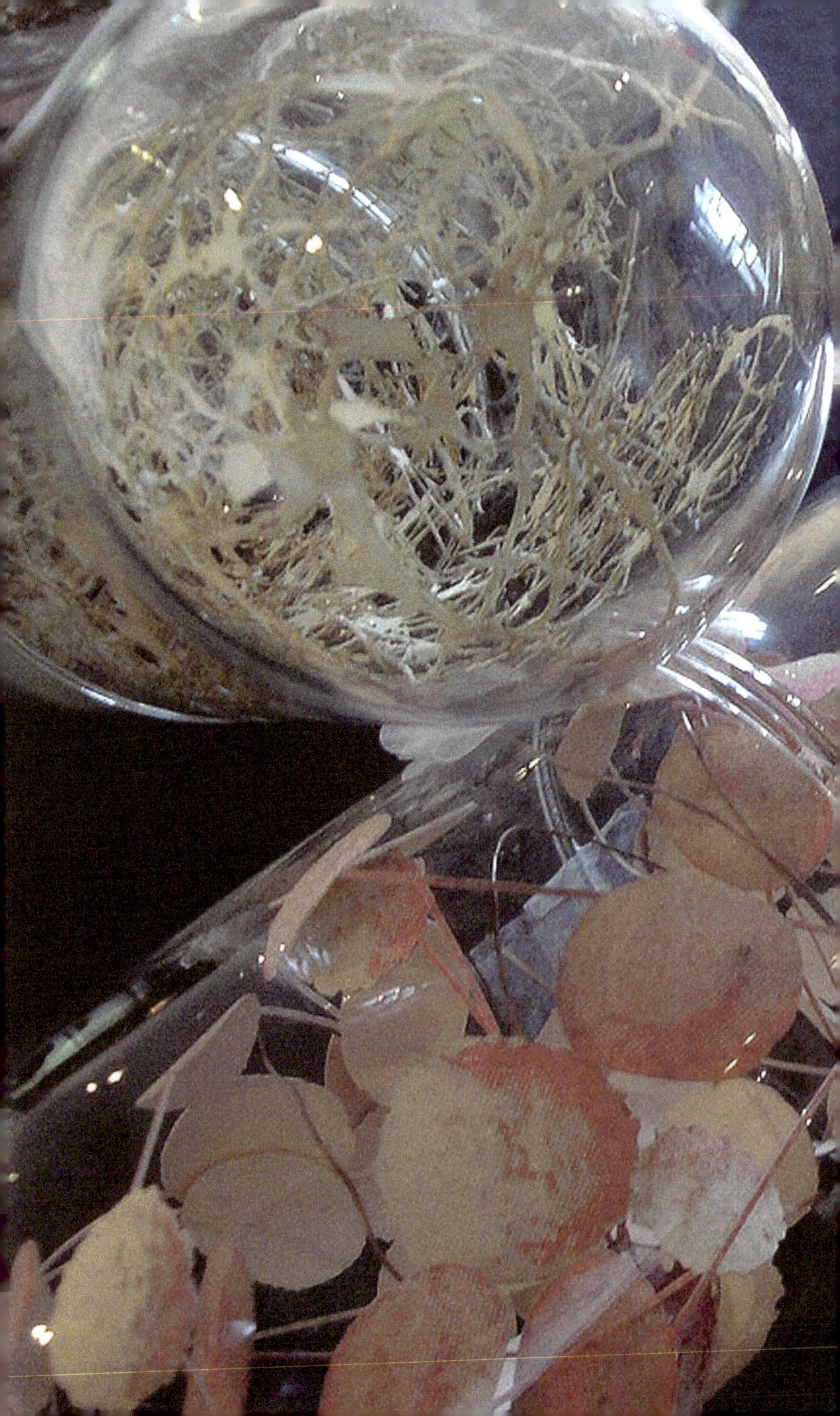

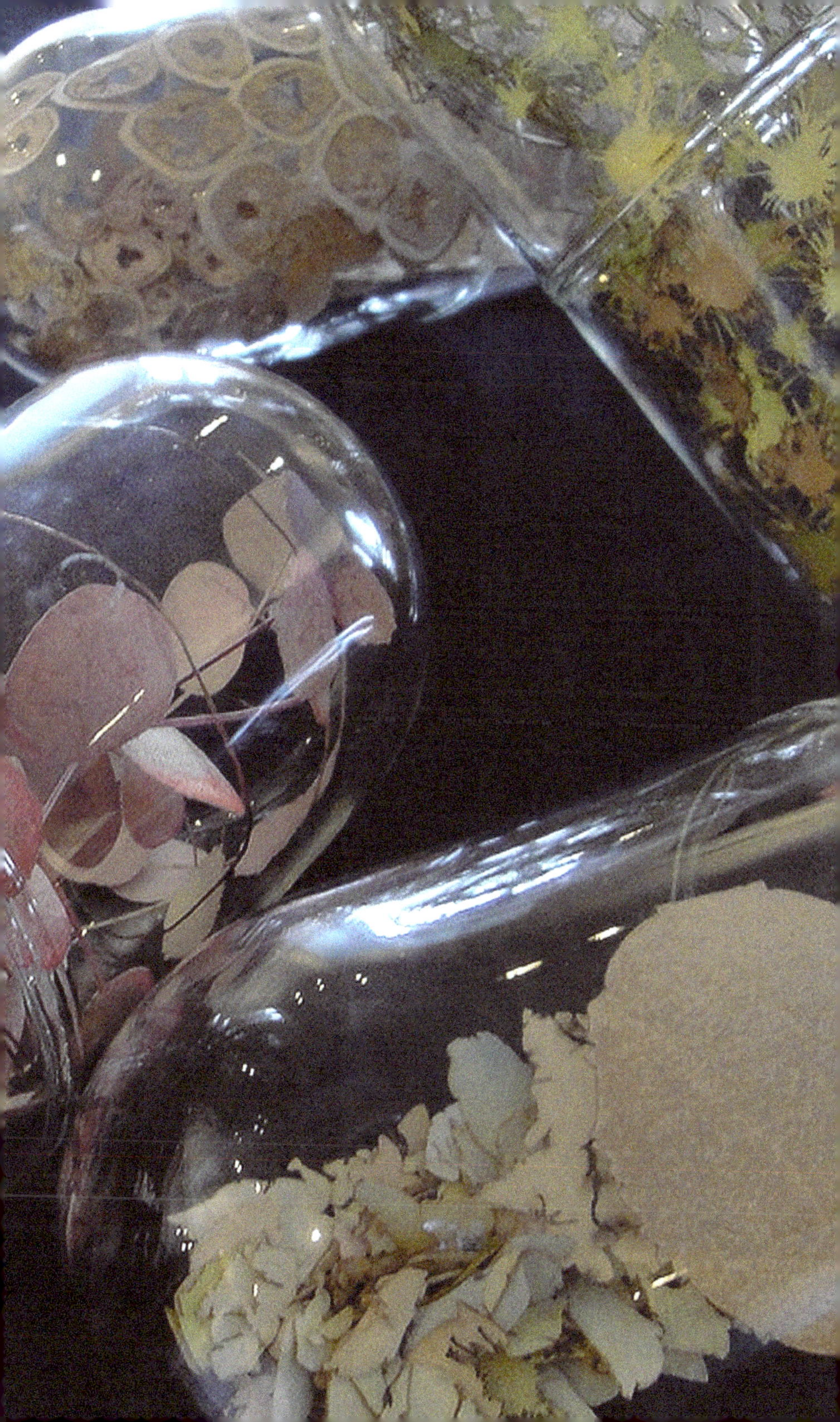

· medicalization of food

Pills implants, cyber

or –

Escape/Remain

Going off your meds

slip someone a mickey

hide it under your tongue

ll

pill heads

pill popper

blue beanies "Yellow Submarine"

Pills

"we're not candy" public serv

to swallow

pill BOX (hats)

letter to a collective

EXPECTING YOU WITH PLEASURE (LOVE)

annie heckman

I love art and I love books. So in addition to my practice as an artist, I founded StepSister Press. When I started publishing books back in 2007, I was constantly guarding my studio practice. I carefully policed the boundary between my publishing and artmaking and tried my best to keep them quite separate.

At some point this tension, combined with other changes at StepSister Press, made it almost impossible for me to produce books. So when Rebecca wrote to us about this project I wondered whether I could keep my roles in line: I wanted to be able to simply shake hands, decide on a smooth editing schedule, and say "Please send me all images formatted CMYK at 300 dpi." But instead, every time Rebecca and I met, I became more

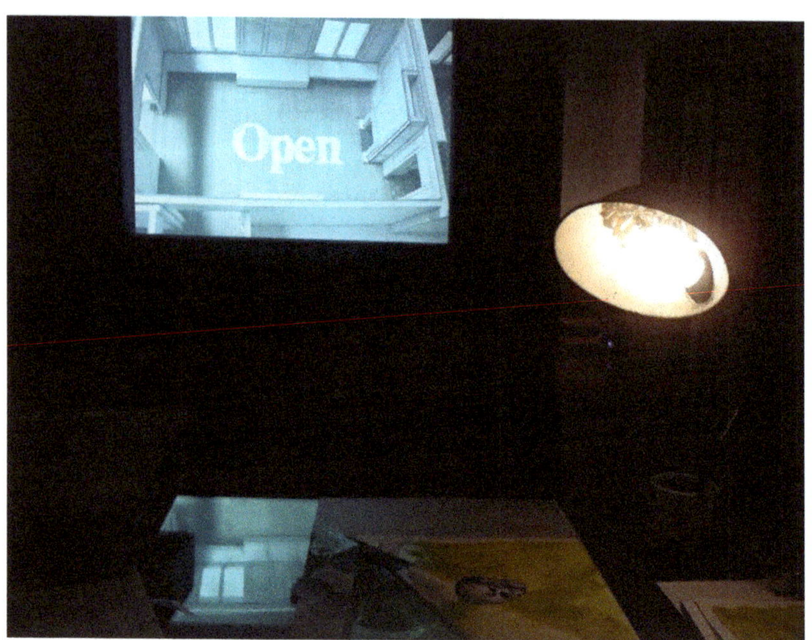

Annie Heckman, *Open*, 2011
animation projection, works on paper, furniture from the International Museum of Surgical Science collection

and more curious about the inner workings of the project, about Rebecca and her many collaborators. I soon found myself in the thick of it.

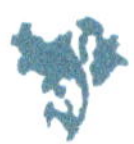

In late 2011, I sat at a desk in the International Museum of Surgical Science, flanked by a brain-like crenelated gold-leaf sculpture in a bell jar and an animated projection I was making, based on a 1953 film of a trephination performed in Peru using ancient Incan tools. Across the room was a display case filled with skulls showing various outcomes of early surgery, along with samples of the types of tools used in the film. Drawings and cut-out photographs cluttered the desk, along with two manila file folders, one of them containing thin, faded sheets of detailed typed correspondences between various surgeons writing to Max Thorek, the founder of the museum. A weathered telegram caught my eye:

EXPECTING YOU AND SIMY WITH PLEASURE STOP.
PLEASURE is crossed off, replaced in large written letters with LOVE.

When I first started the animation, I had been concerned about having too superficial a take on the personality of the doctor in the film, wondering how I could get past the bloody images to understand him. Suddenly, I'm not worried anymore.

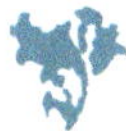

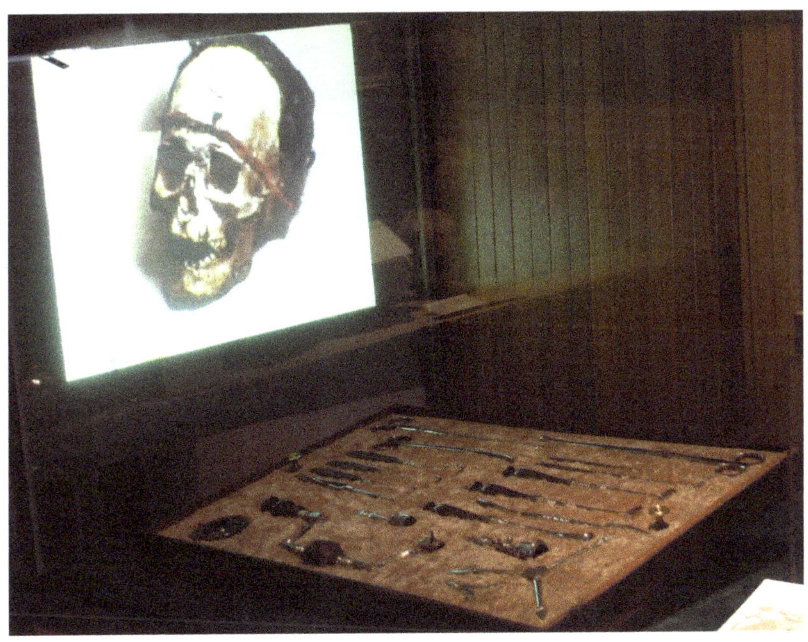

Erin Obradovich, 1953 trephination film from the International Museum of Surgical Science archives transferred to video and projected, 2011, installation integrated into early surgery display
photo Rebecca Keller

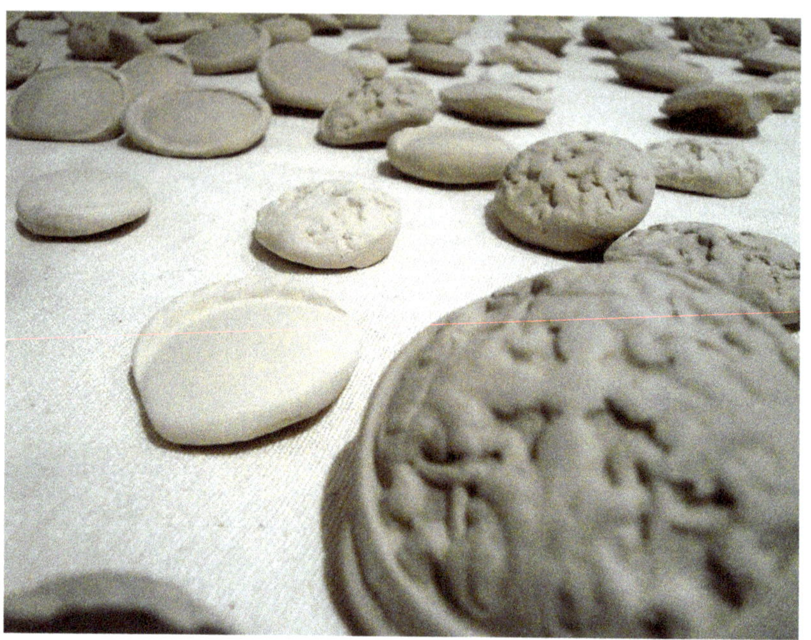

Amber Ginsburg, *Knob* (detail), 2011
porcelain
In the museum's bathrooms, Ginsburg's piece explored the curious habits people develop to avoid touching doorknobs in public bathrooms after washing their hands. Using porcelain, a material often associated with hygienic spaces, and terms collected from visitors, Ginsburg illustrated historical theories of contagion.
photo Andrew Ginger

I can't remember when the members of the collective and I started tossing around the word "love" in correspondence. I think we started to sign emails like that around fall of 2010, and a search for the word "love" in my emails with Rebecca reveals 48 hits. But these warm personal connections aren't coincidental, just as the correspondence between those two doctors isn't a side note to the creation of this museum. These warm ties of mutual support are the required conditions for this type of art to be made, a set of conditions that Rebecca cultivates skillfully. My experience with these artists has left me with a new set of impressions about what collaboration can be.

Erin Obradovich (who handed me a protein bar the first time I met her because I was looking hungry, and then lent me

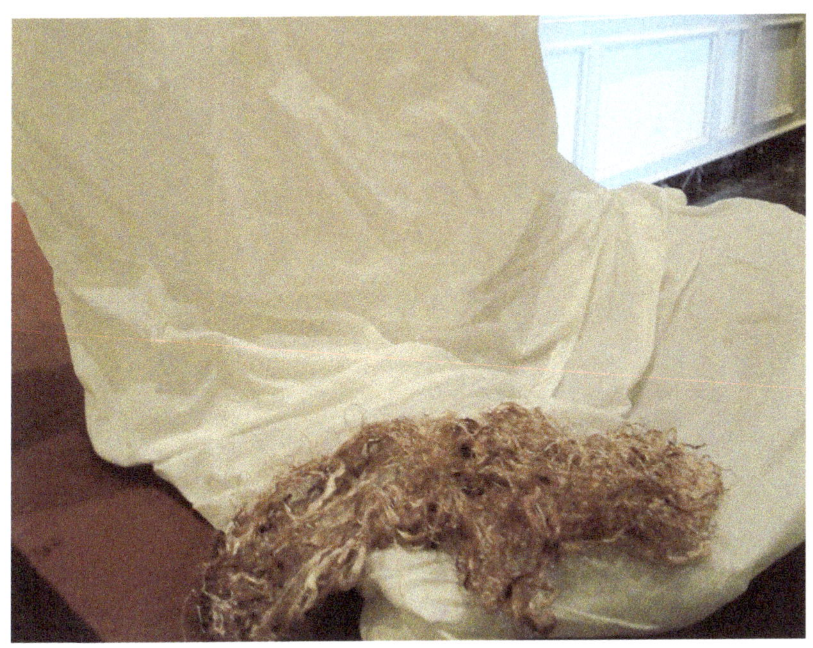

Maral Hashemi, *A Heart Like Yours and A Heart Like Mine, Panegyric for Murray H. Kwon MD*, 2011
foam board, paper, cotton, glue, rolf, silk thread, artist's blood
Murray H. Kwon, a Cardiothoracic surgeon performed a life-saving operation on Hashemi's father. She created this piece in response.
photo Andrew Ginger

her car to drive to the store for installation odds and ends) uncovered the trephination film that would be the basis for my project. Her project of unearthing and recontextualizing footage and audio from the museum's archives has reinvigorated the space, giving it the feel of multiple micro-eras overlapping in historic specificity and richness.

Amber Ginsburg (who made me part of her Art Theory Summer Camp, whose dissection of Bruno Latour and Buckminster Fuller inspired me to go back into college teaching) took on the topic of contagion via the museum's lavatories. She skillfully folding this inquiry into her practice by recasting doorknobs into porcelain gems for visitors to take and by spelling out the many forms of contagion on the walls of the museum's third-floor individual bathrooms using raw unfired clay.

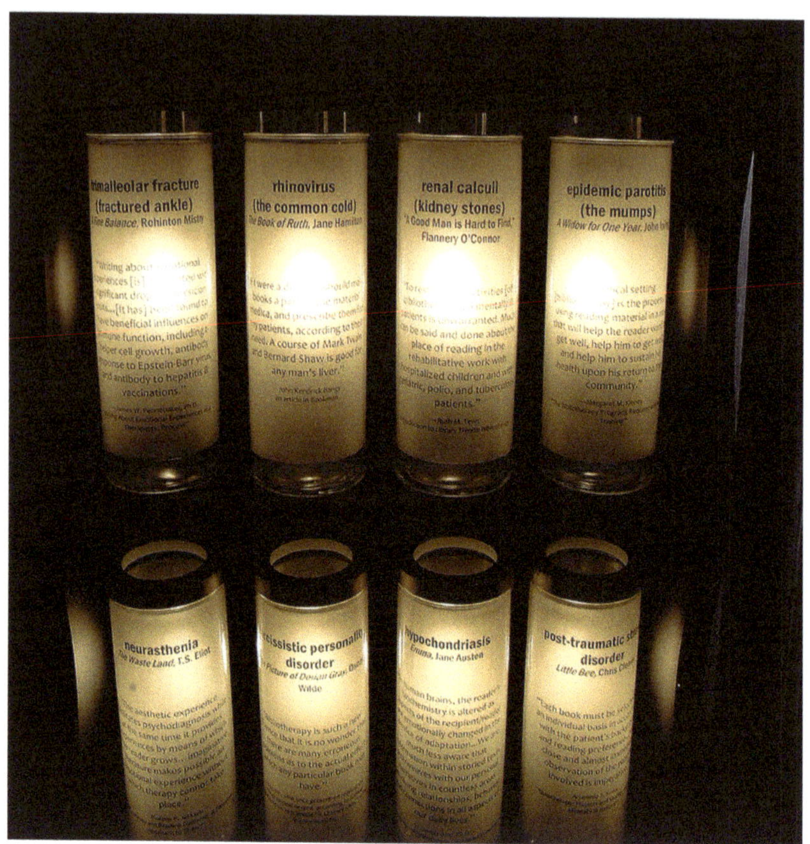

Kristin Ginger, *Fiction of the Body* (detail), 2011
This modern apothecary stall prescribed bibliographical citations of literature as remedies for common physical and mental maladies, challenging the popular conviction that only ingestion or injection of a physical substance can cause healing.
photo Andrew Ginger

Maral Hashemi (who greeted me at the door of the International Museum of Surgical Science for my first collective meeting, and introduced me to the work of Manly Palmer Hall) created a tactile panegyric to a doctor, thanking him for saving her father's life by stitching the text in her own blood. Her investigations in the exhibit wove personal experience, anatomical research, and mysticism.

Kristin Ginger (who brought extra snacks to the reading, who will now become my Devanagari study buddy, and who shared the most pointed writing on postpartum psychosis I have ever experienced) intervened throughout the space with her poetry bombs and set up an apothecary book dispensing bibliotherapeutic prescriptions in the museum's stately library. Her work opened the door for a more literary perspective on the research processes that infused all the artists' practices, for example with a reading circle event in the space.

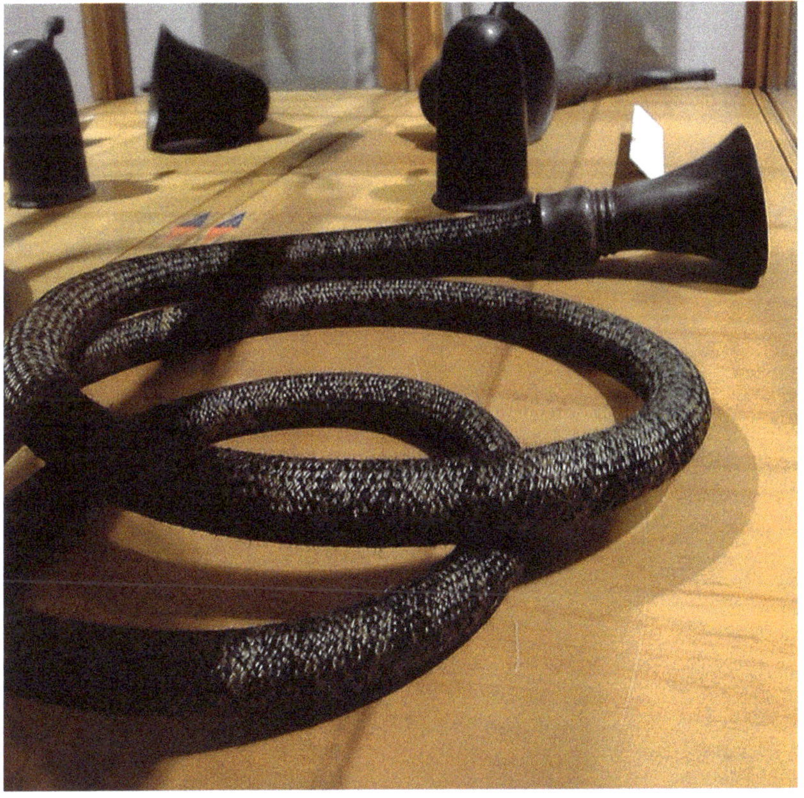

Joseph G. Cruz
"If a tree falls...?", 2011
museum hearing aids, sounds from audio perception research, audio equipment, museum bench
This project incorporated a chronological display of the technological advancements of hearing aids. A sound installation using files from recent audio perception research, played amidst these artifacts. *"If a tree falls...?"* asked viewers, "What do we do with these electrical signals once they reach the auditory brainstem?"
photo Andrew Ginger

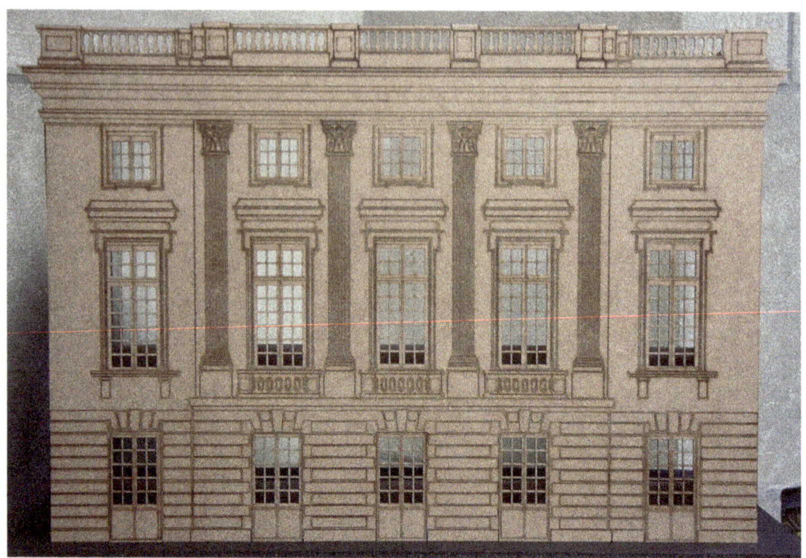

Liene Bosque, *Marie Antoinette's Petit Home*, 2011
laser cut on MDF, 22 x 9.5 x 15 inches
photo Annie Heckman

Joseph G. Cruz (who managed to find my favorite passage in *Proust was a Neuroscientist*, whose project formed the audio backdrop for my entire experience animating on the third floor) organized a chronology of the technology of hearing aids and then deftly investigated the relationship of audio input and processing in his accompanying sound installation.

Liene Bosquê (who first pulled me from Skype hinterlands as I searched for collective members during an online meeting, who shared her research on the building's history with me, who helped to document my piece during the opening) created comparative, architectural models of the museum itself, also known as the Countiss mansion, and its inspiration, Marie Antoinette's Petit Trianon.

Briana Schweizer (who designed the postcards for the show, spotted me ten dollars, and told amazing stories about her work in the film world) created several skillful interventions in the space, including a digital recreation of Napoleon's mask using her own face, and delicious chill

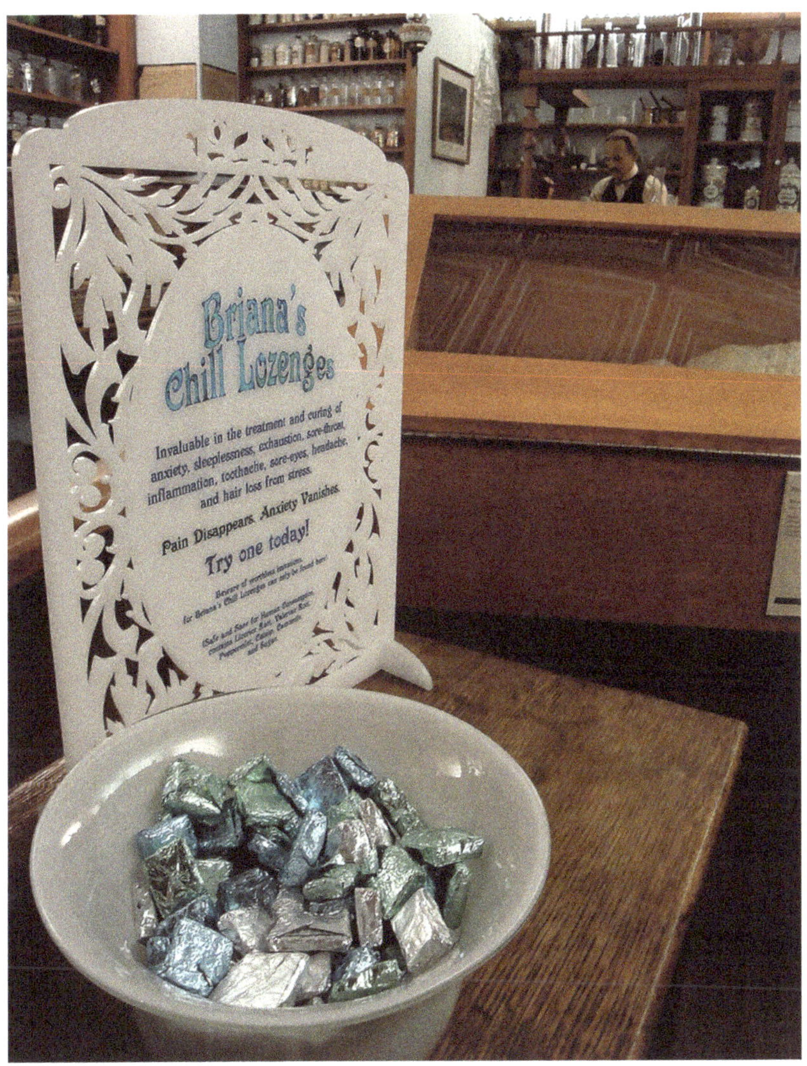

Briana Schweizer, *Briana's Chill Lozenges*, 2011
herbs, sugar, foil wrappers, acrylic, glass

pills in the apothecary complete with snake-oil sales pitches. Briana's work showed a thorough research process with her subjects of interest as well as with the most current use of technology in crafting her pieces.

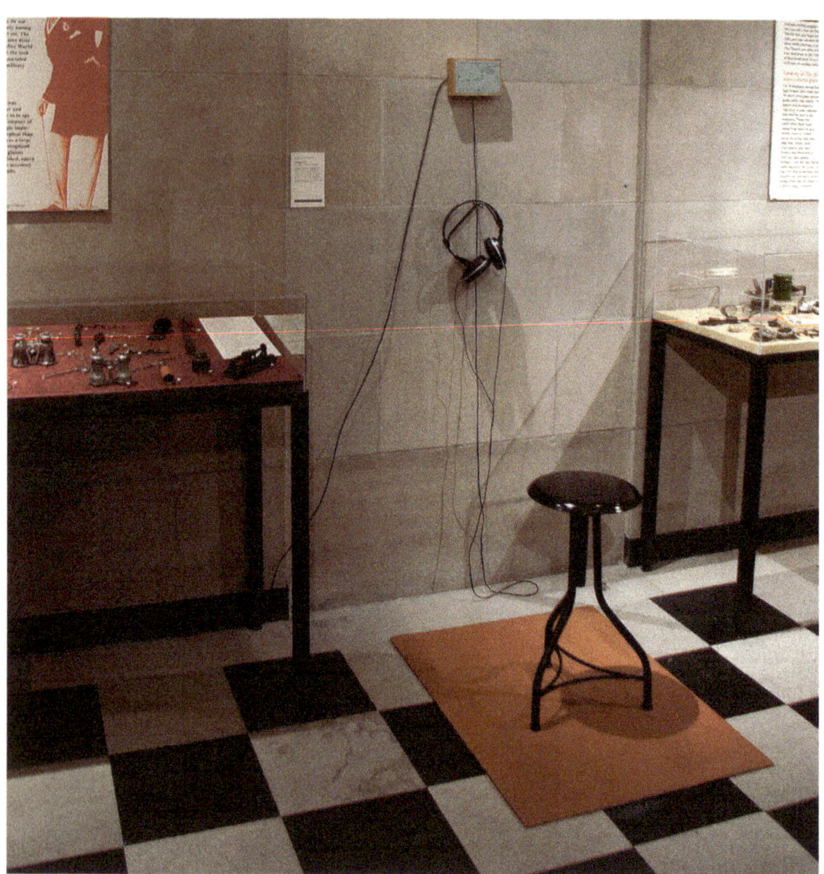

Rebecca Hernandez, *Tonic*, 2011
photo Annie Heckman

Rebecca Hernandez (who fed me delicious soup, discussed meditation with me, created all the wall labels for the exhibit, and took the lead in organizing a presentation on herbalism that has transformed my kitchen from a wasteland into a potion room) pulled from the shared auditory experiences of a hospital, the humming and beeping of numerous machines, to create a meditative soundtrack through which, sharply and intuitively, we can understand that every situation is workable.

Elise Goldstein (who introduced me to etching, Baltimore, and Rebecca) and Meredith Zielke (who allowed me to sift through her tools for hours on end) collaborated on two videos, rendering Elise's performance through her poetic documentary

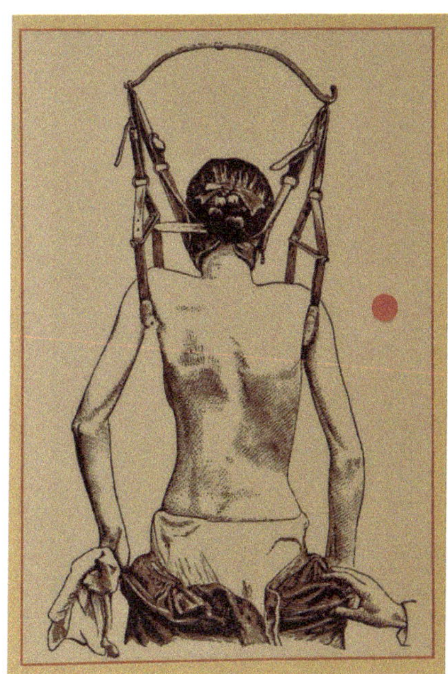

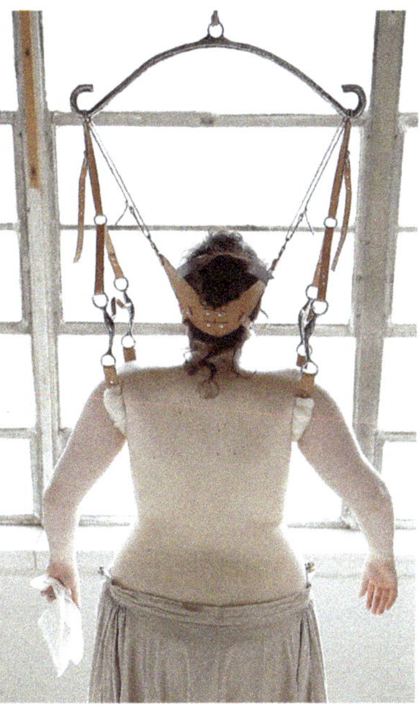

Elise Goldstein and Meredith Zielke, *This Is All I Can Offer*, 2011
video installation
photo Meredith Zielke

sensibility. Together they recreated a traction device and the conditions in which it would have been used, crafting a video installed in the tiny doorway off the spinal surgery section of the museum. When I felt the familiar nauseous ripple in the back of my legs that normally only happens when I consider gross injury to myself or family, their piece forced me to question how often I use the clinical presentation of medical knowledge as a safe censor for my ego.

Rebecca Keller (who brought me into this project, listened to my growing pains for the first half of every book meeting we had, and instigated this entire group of young artists in the exploration of historic sites) rightly balanced her work in the spheres of reverence and comedy. If you would like to contemplate the sense of immortality with which doctors are imbued, Rebecca's interventions in the Hall of Immortals adorn the sculptures of famous doctors with their respective attributes, right down to Pasteur's rabbits and Lister's coal tar soap. But walk a

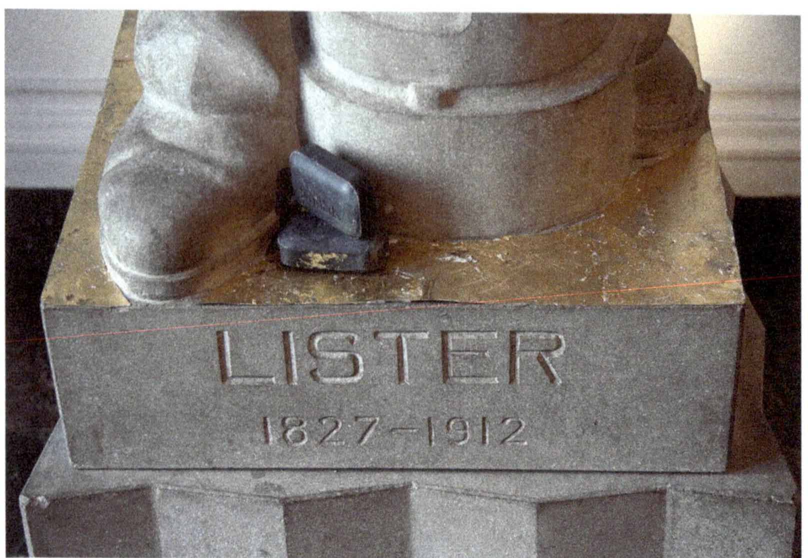

Rebecca Keller, *Attributes of the Gods: Lister*, 2011
gold leaf, coal tar soap
Keller's Attributes of the Gods plays with the idea of doctor-as-God by adding to the statues of famous healers in the Museum's Hall of Immortals relevant "attributes"—a term that refers to symbolic objects in images of saints—made from materials ranging from chlorinated lime to papyrus to coal tar.

bit further and your eyes will flash on small cards scrawled with raunchy doctor jokes tucked into corners of the museum. What could open things up more for her collective, than to explore the extremes of the space, to allow her attitude to flash on the most serious and hilarious aspects of a project simultaneously.

Which brings me to my final point. I have had the privilege of making this book with Rebecca and these amazing creative practitioners for almost three years, and the collective has continued to grow. Now I get to see what happens next. EXPECTING YOU WITH PLEASURE (LOVE).

right: Rebecca Keller, *Distillery of Knowledge*, 2011
laboratory glass, copper wire, copper tubing
In the library, it is clear that medical information grows and develops as each researcher takes into account what came before, and tried to add to it: literally re-searching. This installation uses laboratory glass beakers and distillers to underscore the precariousness of this process.
following spreads: Rebecca Keller, *Attributes of the Gods: Veselius*, 2011
gold leaf, anatomy books from Museum collection
Rebecca Keller, *Did You Hear the One About...*, 2011, ink on mourning stationery

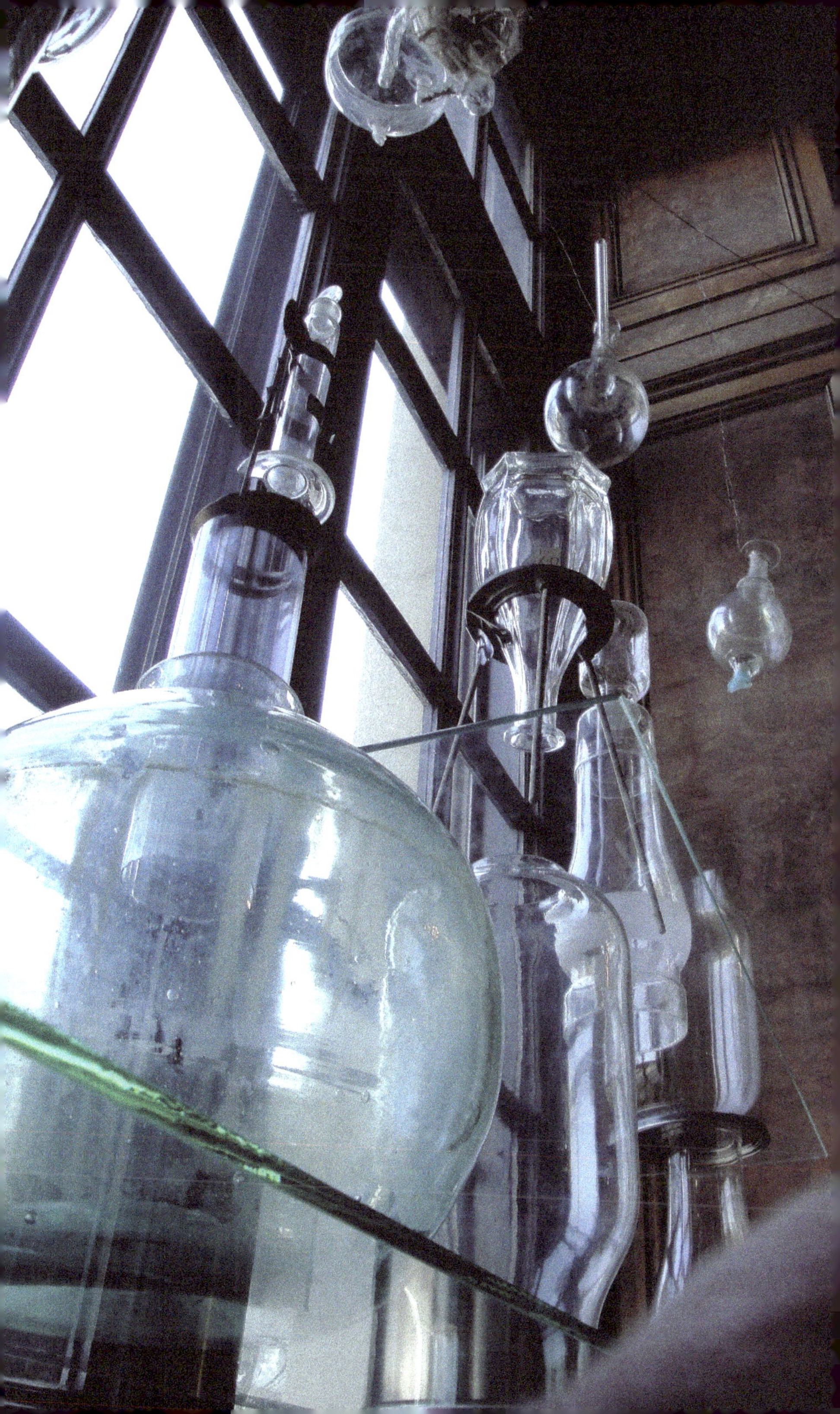

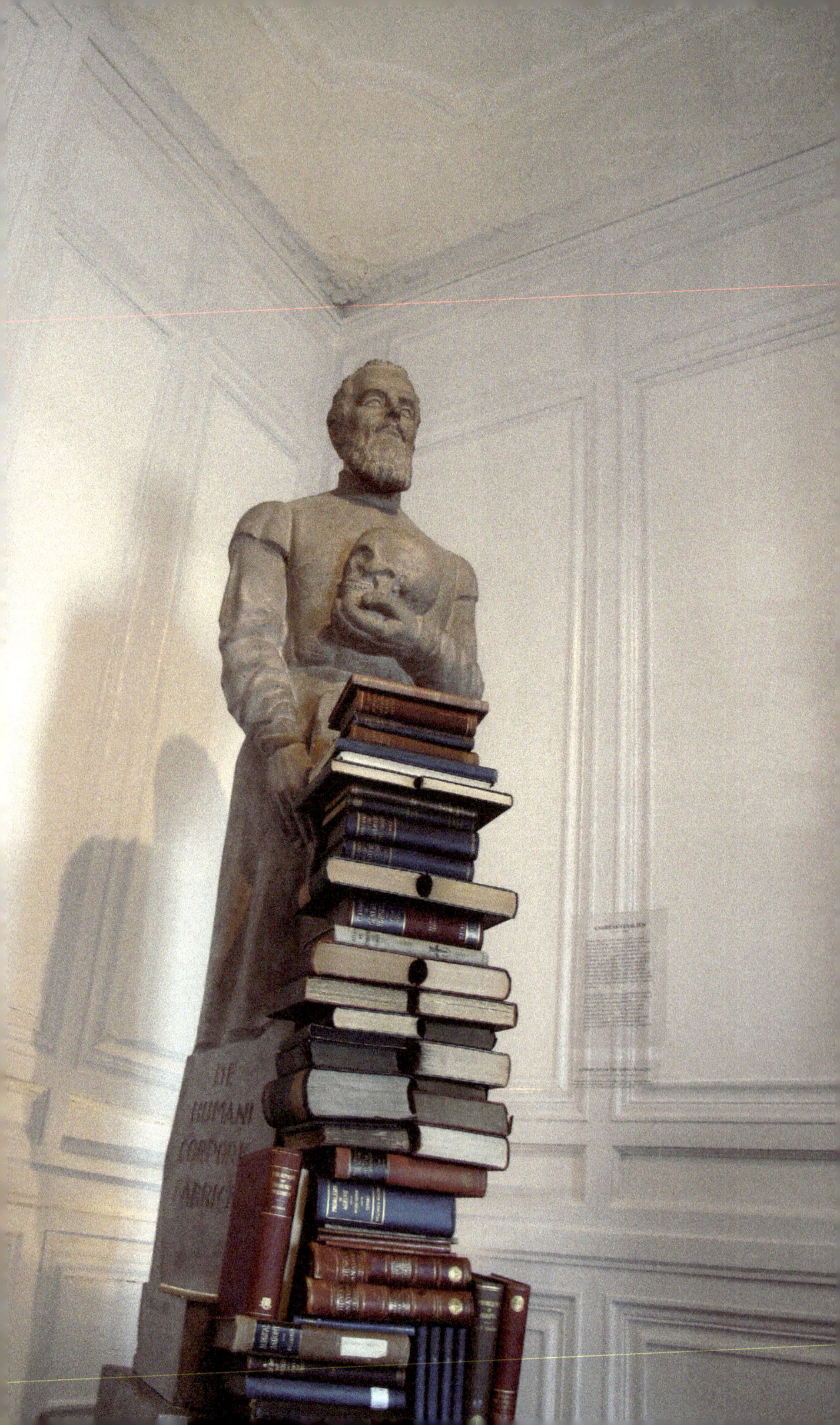
DE
HUMANI

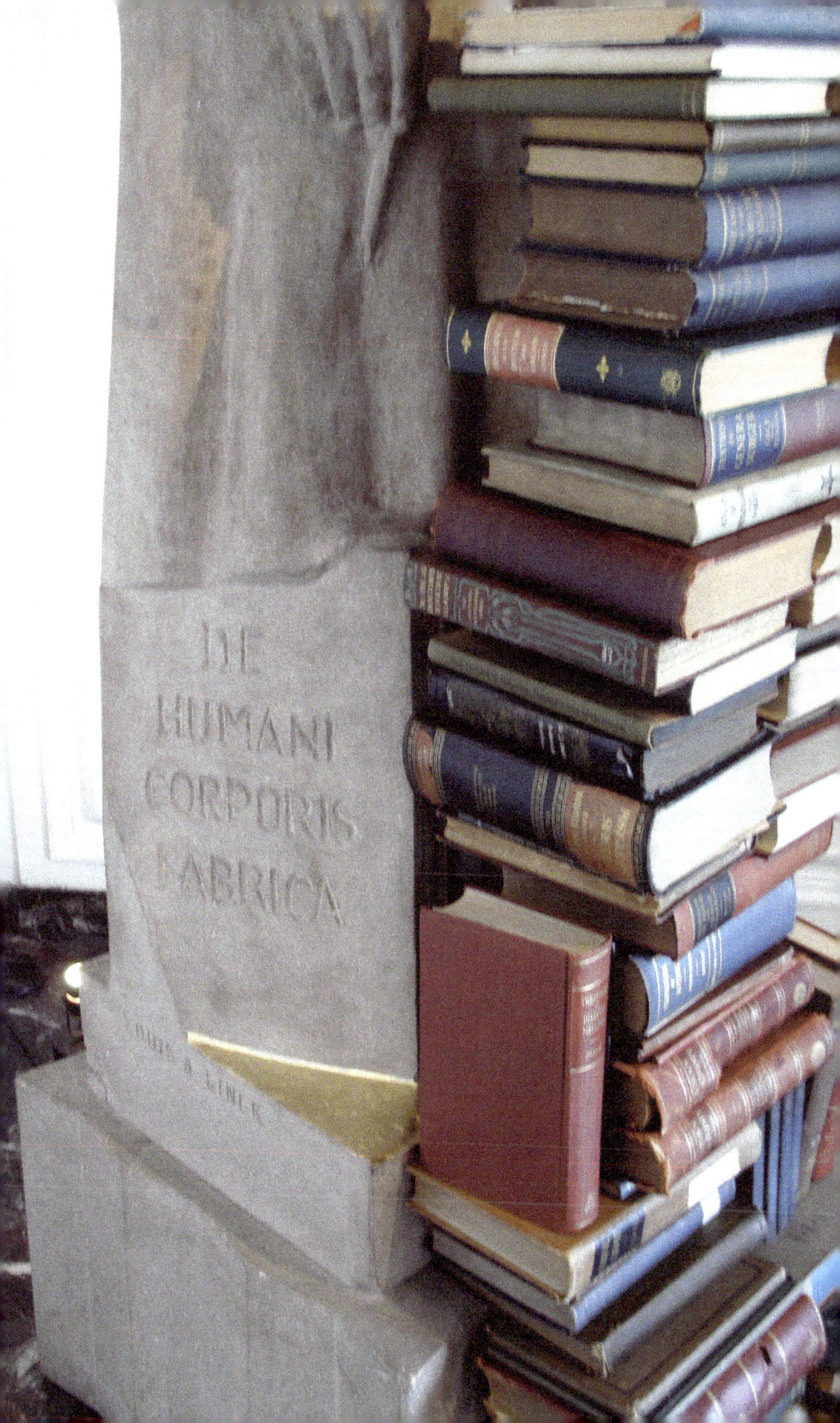
DE
HUMANI
CORPORIS
FABRICA

Doctor: "I
news

Patient: "O

Doctor: "Yo
and A

Patient "Wil
hav

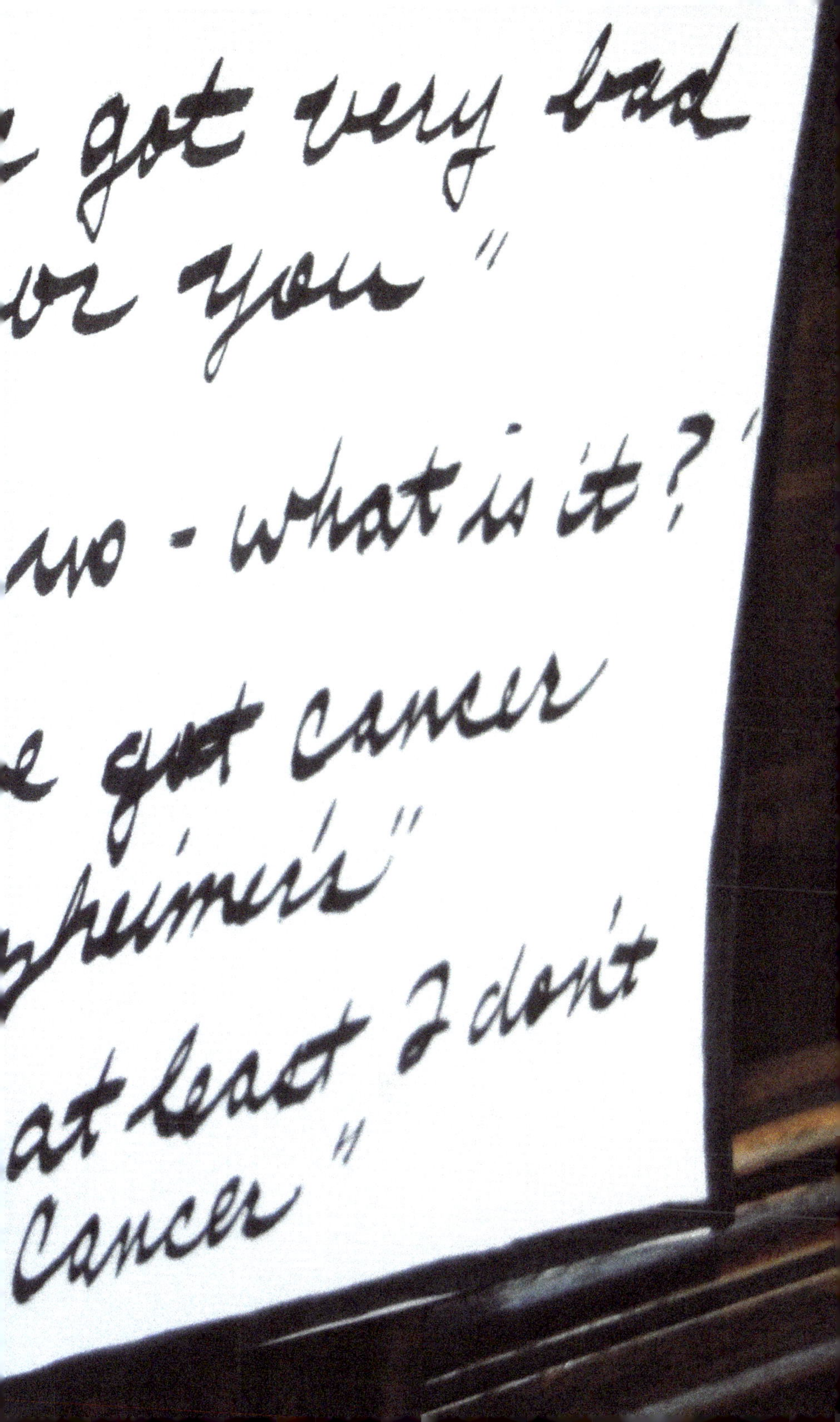

e got very bad
or you"

no - what is it?"

e got cancer
zheimer's"
at least I don't
cancer"

calendar of pills

pillow talk

Tylenol murders

adulterated pills

cocaine turning people's skin black

poppers

take a pill to make it go away

↑ medical equivalent of waving a magic wand

Things for inside u

- Cockroaches
- razor wire

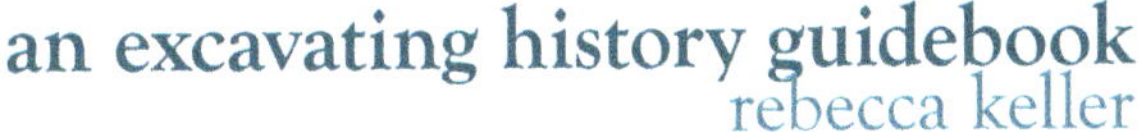

an excavating history guidebook

rebecca keller

finding a space

This is probably the most daunting task. Begin with research. Remember, research can start with walking, with eyes and brain and intuition open. Keep in mind that a historic site is not only the mansion down the road. It can also be a school, a hospital, cemetery, park, department store, or field house.

All of the above offer tantalizing possibilities. For example, schools, hospitals and parks all are sites where well-researched larger histories (the history of public education, histories of medicine/technology/sport, etc.) intersect with local narratives and stories (economic situations, civil rights, technological advances, accidents, epidemics). What happened at the local swimming pool during the polio epidemic? When did the area hospital become integrated? What is the oldest piece of equipment in it? Does the school still have a mimeograph machine? How did it work? Can it be used?

Realize you—or your group—may have more resources than you are aware of. Perhaps someone's grandfather funded the old orphanage. Maybe someone is a collector of train memorabilia, and knows people who maintain old station houses. Someone's uncle may be the director or a volunteer at an historical society. Identify a few possibilities or places that you are curious about.

Talk to people. This process is largely one of relationship building. There needs to be a sense of trust. Try to look at it from the point of view of the manager(s) of the site you'd like to use. What would you worry about, if you were in their shoes? What could be the possible benefits to them? (A sense of community involvement? Telling a little known story? Greater public profile? Fulfilling their mission to serve a community?)

Perhaps a phased approach would make the most sense. Step One is simply asking to take photos, do research, explore potential. After getting a sense of what sort of work could be generated, the person in charge of the site could be provided with formal proposals, drawings to discuss phase two—creating an actual exhibition or intervention at the site.

the artmaking

Let's say you have a site identified and approval secured. What now?

It is an iterative process. Spend some time in the space. It is a good idea to have undertaken some research before hand—to identify possible areas of interest—general themes if not specifics.

As you walk through the place, keep an eye out for opportunities. Bring a camera and a sketchbook. What catches your eyes or imagination? Are there little niches that could serve as display areas, almost as cases, for a diorama or small vignette?

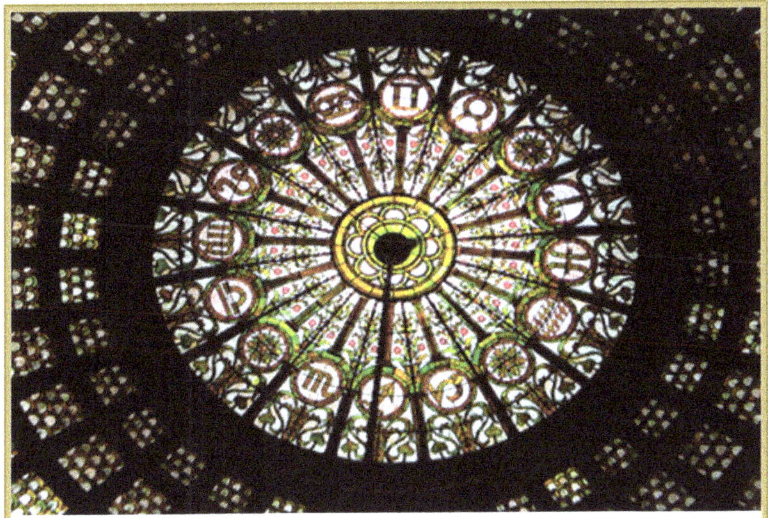

Excavating History: Chicago Loop

OPEN HOUSE
THE CHICAGO CULTURAL CENTER
Pedway Studio in the lower level
at Randolph St. just west of Michigan Avenue
Monday, April 27, 3-6pm

The School of The Art Institute Of Chicago's
EXCAVATING HISTORY COLLABORATIVE

In recognition of the centennial of Daniel Burnham's plan, the artists in this exhibition have been conducting research into the complex histories of Chicago's Loop then generating artworks in response. The collective has been in residence at the pedway studio of the Chicago Cultural center. The resulting exhibition includes work that reference the way fire is encoded in the city landscape, the Chicago River and the rhetoric and civic rituals of monument-making.

Come and sample some tasty Chicago-themed treats, and see the results of Excavating History's residence at the Cultural Center's Pedway Studio/ Gallery.

Special performance at 4pm.

design by Briana Schweizer, 2009

Are there deep window ledges that could be pedestals or vitrines? Are there transoms that could form the "eye" for a camera obscura or a projection? Are there fences that could hold text? Are the rooms too bright for a projection, or too dark for subtle paintings? If an outdoor component tickled someone's fancy—is there access to electricity if need be, or a roof?

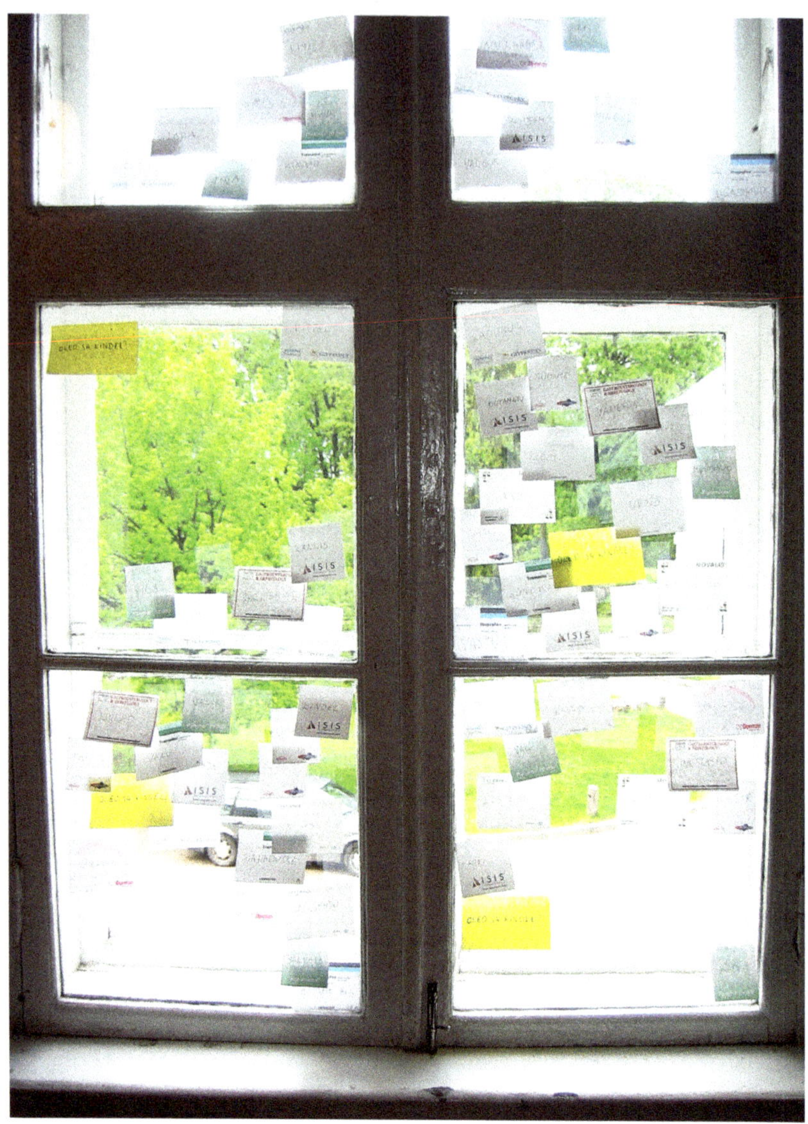

Collaborative installation, 1801 Anatomy Theater, Tartu Estonia, 2006
students' notes, prescription pad, drug company stickie notes on window, 6 x 4 feet

On a less practical level: Are there objects in the collection or spaces that suggest materials, a method, a way to proceed? Be open to the many histories—especially those that are ignored or hidden—the shadow histories—that are suggested by the ones that are highlighted. Be alert to the politics, the social contexts, and the poetic connections presented or suggested by the site. Listen to the language people use to describe the site. There is an official version of why it is important—is that why it is important to you? Or most interesting?

A poet once told me she begins by casting about for an abiding image—and that to court it she tries to "stay down in the dirt" as long as possible. "The dirt" is messy, associative, connection-making, open-ended. Do not self-censor. If it interests you, write it down. If the workers /curators /volunteers /educators /trustees at a site feel it is important, write it down. If a question or quibble occurs to you, write it down. If a physical aspect of the place—the way sound carries, the color, the materials, the objects in it, captures your attention or imagination, write it down.

Do more research. Let things simmer. As I said, this is an iterative process. You begin, visit, research, think, research, visit again—and each time ideas, associations, and hopefully, ideas for possible artworks begin to bubble up. Ideas and themes emerge and begin to cohere. In my experience, this process is made richer and more successful through conversation and collaboration. Mull over possibilities or amazing facts or interesting tidbits with your colleagues/fellow artists. Share photos, passing fancies, research topics, resources.

All of the above said, I have on several occasions been struck with a certainty—an idea lands in my head, fully formed and I know almost exactly what I want to do. Of course, it is always necessary to challenge these ideas. But if they hold up—don't look a metaphorical gift horse in the mouth, and be grateful for such bolts of lightning.

The following terms, descriptions and etymologies are useful for thinking about the discipline we call history, and for finding places of entry, elasticity, or moments for creative engagement. They are meant to be suggestive, to open up associations, to evoke, to prompt.

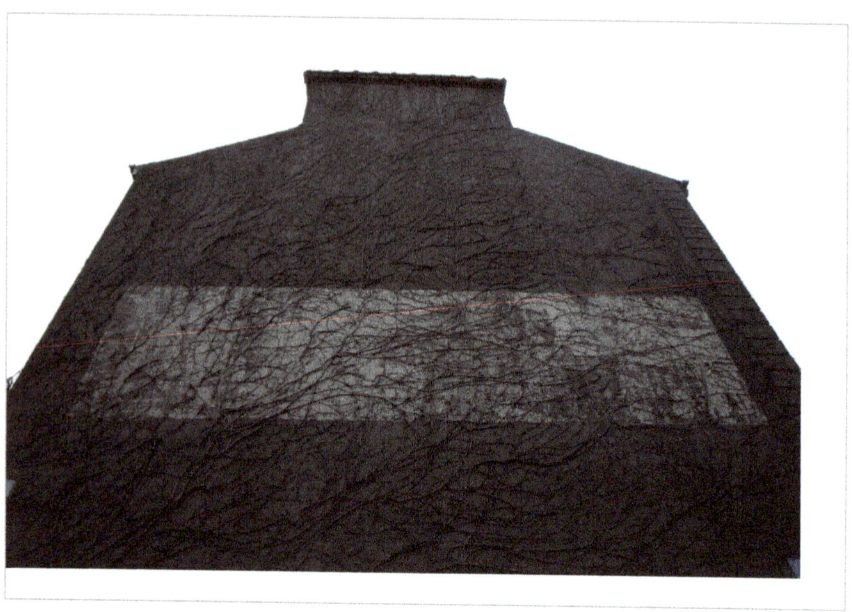

Gilly Youner, *Deeply Vined*, Galway, Ireland, 2011

palimpsest

A palimpsest is a manuscript page, whether from scroll or book, that has been written on, scraped off, and used again. The word "palimpsest" comes through Latin from ("again" + "I scrape").

Additional meanings, all of them interesting and pertinent to *Excavating History* projects, include referring to a plaque that has been turned around and engraved on what was originally the back. There are also double palimpsests on parchment where both sides were written on, scraped, and reused. The term is also used in forensics to establish the sequence of events based on the way objects are placed over one another.

"Palimpsest" has a specific meaning in architecture, referring to a trace that has been left behind, a ghost of what was once there. For example, a building is imprinted by the structure next to it, and when the neighboring structure is demolished we see the discolored brick or faded paint marking the outline of the destroyed building; in the interior, the layout of removed walls or trim or steps can be discerned where the painted wall stops or the floor boards change color.

To me, the term "palimpsest" is an evocative way to think about history. It seems a very accurate description of the way people experience time, that is, as a layering of present experiences over past ones; an interweaving of personal references with place; a series of connections between public events and private meanings; and the ability to see the multiple public, political and social meanings embedded in a single place, simultaneously.

synecdoche

When a part of something refers to the whole thing OR

* when a "whole" is used to refer to a part, OR
* when a specific class of thing is used to refer to more general class of things OR
* its opposite: when a general class of thing is used to refer to a more specific class OR
* when a material is used to refer to an object made from that material.

Phrases in which a part of something is used to refer to the whole:

* "A roof over your head" = house
* "Boots on the ground" = number of soldiers
* "Head count"= number of (presumably complete) people.
* "Wheels"=car

Phrases where the whole of something is used to refer to a part of it:

* "Use your head [brain] to figure it out."
* "Move your feet" = Get your body moving.
* "The United States moved to..." = the government of the U.S. acted.

Examples in which a specific kind of thing is used to refer to a more general kind:

* Vaseline for petroleum jelly, or Kleenex for tissue
* Castle for home
* Benedict Arnold for traitor, John Hancock for signature

Examples in which a general class is used to refer to a more specific thing
* "Pet" to refer to all domestic animals
* "Truck" to refer to tractor trailers, pick-ups, jeeps, etc.

Phrases where the material from which an object is made refers to the object itself:
* "Tinkle the ivories" ivories = piano keys
* "Pay with plastic" plastic = credit card

WHY are synecdoches useful to think about? Because they objectify—give solid and concrete examples for—larger concepts. For an *Excavating History* project, artists need to distill complex ideas or references into physical objects, or use an object or image to evoke a set of ideas and representations. This is what synecdoches do.

metonymy

Closely related to synecdoche. Metonymy is when an idea or a thing is referred to by the name of something associated with it-- a sort of a grab bag, shorthand way for identifying a whole set of ideas and realities. For example "Washington" refers to a whole set of attitudes and cultures and political power structures because the U.S. Government is centered there. Unlike synecdoche, the relationship is not necessarily direct, but associative.

cenotaph

The word cenotaph literally means empty grave but refers to a monument or a memorial, often with heroic scale or public importance. There are several different kinds of cenotaphs:

(1) A cenotaph memorializes a person whose body was lost or was buried at sea.

(2) A cenotaph memorializes a person who was originally buried at that location, but later the body was moved to a different location

(3) A cenotaph can also simply memorialize a person of note as a gesture of respect and honor. The Washington monument is a major example.

The word cenotaph helps people think about how memorials and monuments are related, and how certain ideas and references can become very abstracted and become symbols onto themselves. A whole range of ideas about history are projected onto or performed in our relationships to these structures.

history

Of course some sort of definition is necessary, and of course, any definition is problematic. But here goes: History is the study of the past, with special attention to the written record as it has unfolded over time. Historians use narrative to relate and examine events and may try to discern patterns of cause and effect or influence. *I am struck by how, in this regard, historians are like novelists or artists.* However, historians make a clear distinction between documented narratives and the unprovable stories common to a particular culture (such as cherished legends like George Washington's chopping down the cherry tree, or the tales of the Knights of the Round Table). These are usually categorized as reflections of a cultural heritage rather than as facts supported by enough documentation that they could be received under the umbrella of History. However, this is a distinction artists or fiction writers don't necessarily feel impelled to honor.

Obviously, no one can escape the influence of their own historical moment, their own spot on the timeline (if we visualize time in a linear way, which is problematic in itself). Because of this, the work of historians is often revisited and re-evaluated by later thinkers or researchers, and the version of history presented at various moments is analyzed from a different perspective.

Historians may use all sorts of records: what is written or documented, what was or is said, as well as what remains of the material culture of the past. Obviously, disciplines like economics, politics, geography, science, and medicine

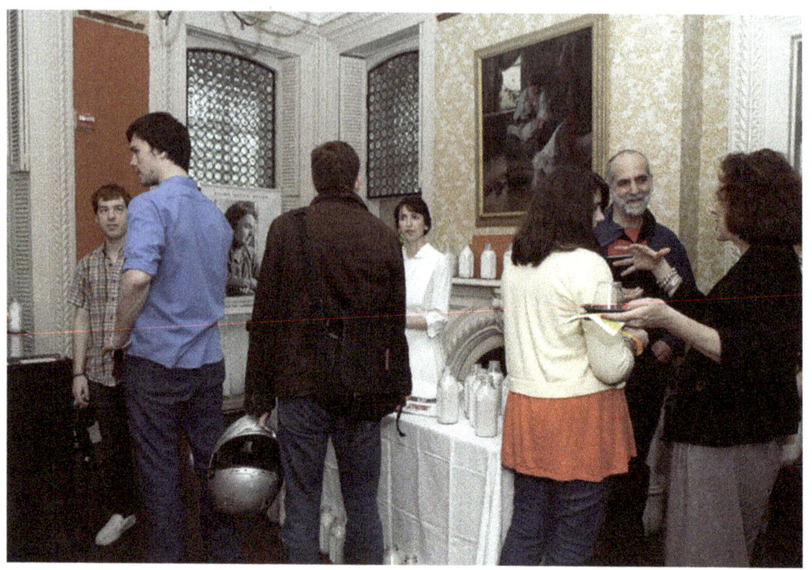

Maral Hashemi, *Elixir of Life*, 2010
during *Messing With Jane* reception at the Jane Addams Hull-House Museum

all have their own specific histories, and also contribute to our understandings of the past in various ways, offering us lenses or philosophies through which to interpret the historic record.

Every work of history implies a judgment of what parts of the record represent most accurately a particular moment in the past, and which do not.

monument, memorial, archive

What is the relationship of memory to history?

How are memory and history made manifest: archive, memorial, monument?

These are three ways that memory and history are objectified, made public and accessible. What are the differences between them? How do they function? How are they accessed differently? Do audiences approach them with different expectations and needs? Obviously, they occupy different kinds of cultural space, and make different types of demands on us.

sasha and zamani

The concepts of Sasha and Zamani[1] are two ways of thinking about time in some Eastern and Central African Cultures. They are also sometimes used to describe states of being (people), and are bound up with memory, death, and ancestors. Clearly, cultural notions of time and the relation of the living (present) time to the time of one's ancestors are complex. But the concepts are enormously compelling in the framework they provide for thinking about history.

Roughly speaking, people can be divided into the living, the Sasha and the Zamani. The recently dead—who have friends and relatives and acquaintances who are still alive, and for whom they live on in memory—are Sasha. When the last person with whom their life overlapped dies, they pass into Zamani. As Zamani, they are among the more generalized (and revered) ancestors.

But the concepts run deeper than categorizing people in reference to their lived state. They are ontological categories and provide ways of thinking about time. The present and immediate past, but also the short-term future—are Sasha. Sasha can be said to roughly correspond to events that have recently taken place, are still active, or will take place within the next few months.

When an event is realized it moves out of Sasha, and is absorbed into Zamani. Sasha and Zamani dimensions overlap. As events pass through Sasha time they become Zamani. Zamani encompasses all the past—it is capacious and stretches to hold both mythological pasts and creations as well as heroes, ancestors, and stories. It is history but also prehistory. It could also be seen as the sea of time itself.

In both of these ways—the understanding that stories may change when there is no longer anyone alive who witnessed the original event, thus passing into a different type of history

---

1. I first read about this concept in relation to historical research in *Lies My Teacher Told Me: Everything Your American History Textbook Got Wrong*, by James W. Loewen, 1996, Touchstone Books.

or memory—and the idea of a historic past that is side by side with myth and remembrance— are rich with possibility for thinking about the rhetoric of historic sites and how we intersect with and think about them.

thought problem / exercise

Tell me a story about something that happened to you but that you don't remember.

* First, tell it to me as if you want to impress me with something about you.
* Then, tell it to me to show me something about the time it took place.
* Then, tell it to me to show me something about another person in the story. First, to make them look bad. Then, to make them look good.

Elise Goldstein, *The Ink Well*, 2010
photo Emerson Granillo

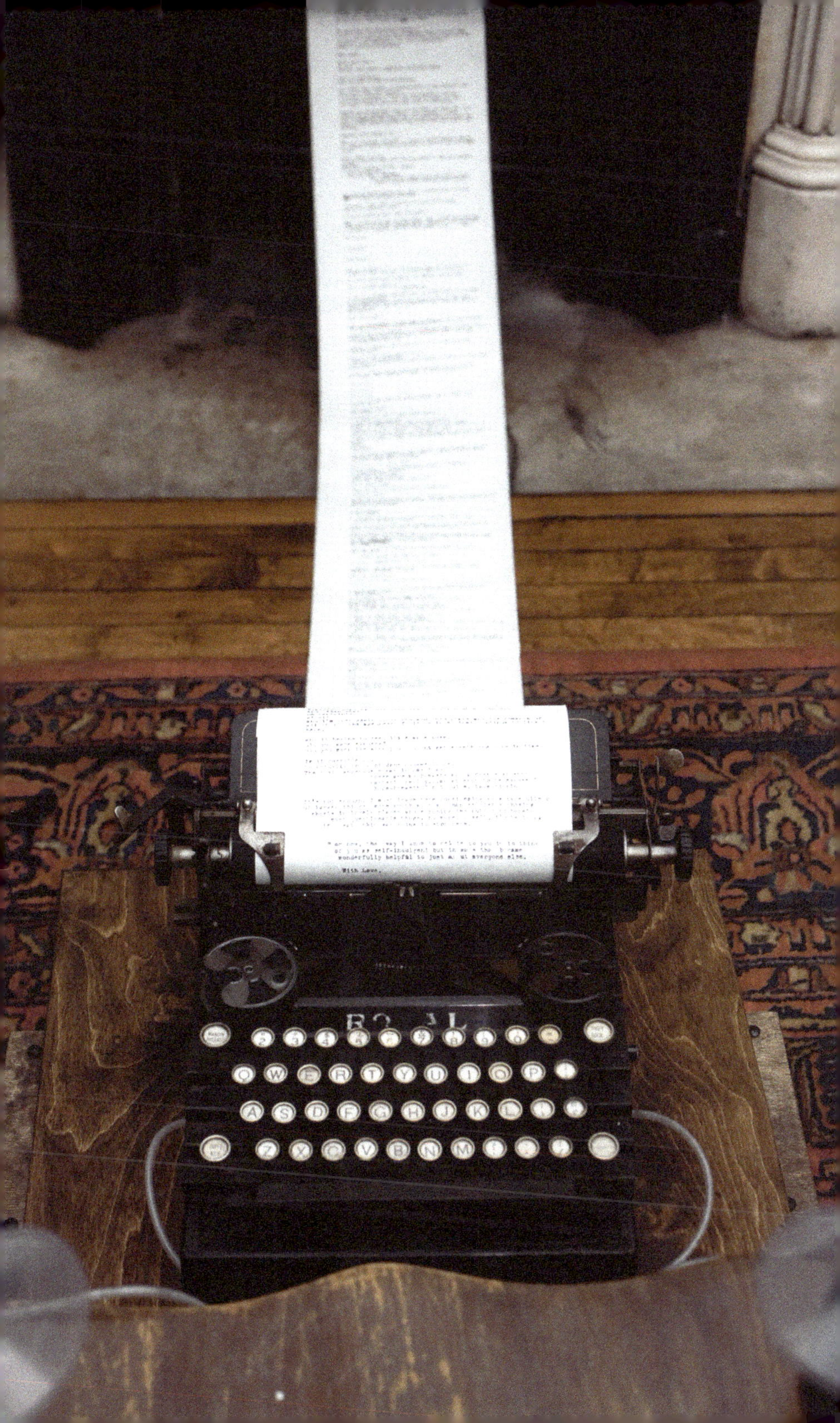
With Love,

deadline - to

images of notes

print delivery
deadline

contributor biographies

Rebecca Keller is an artist, researcher and writer with a strong background in museum education and curating. Honors include two Fulbrights, grants from the National Endowment for the Arts; the Illinois Arts Council; the College Art Association; the Grainger Foundation and the Anne Vogt Fuller /Marion Titus Searle Fellowship in Interdisciplinary Arts at the Ragdale Foundation. She was named as an American Association of Museums International Fellow, and in that capacity worked in museums in Sao Paulo and Recife, Brasil. She has exhibited her artwork widely, and has written for a variety of museums and journals. Keller also writes fiction, and has been published in literary journals and nominated for a push-cart prize.

In addition to her ongoing Excavating History projects, Keller is a founding co-editor of *YoYo Magazine.Org*: an iterative, collaborative on-line journal designed to create a platform where creative people can encounter and respond to one another. *Yo-Yo* aims to be connective tissue between community-based, studio-based and site-dependent art practices; between fiction, poetry, essays and nonfiction; between art and literature, and hybrid forms of cultural production.

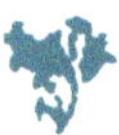

Vincent L. Michael, Ph.D. is the John H. Bryan Chair in Historic Preservation at the School of the Art Institute of Chicago, where he directed the Master of Science in Historic Preservation program from 1996 to 2010. He is a Trustee of the National Trust for Historic Preservation, serves on the Board of Landmarks Illinois and the Global Heritage Fund. He is Chair Emeritus of the National Council for Preservation Education, and among other positions.

Vince has lectured on historic preservation, architecture, geography, art and history throughout the United States, Europe and Asia and his writings include articles in *Design Issues*, *Future Anterior*, *Traditional Building* and *Journal of the Society of Architectural Historians*, a weekly blog *Time Tells* since 2005 and Marfa Public Radio's weekly program *Preservation Nation*.

Vincent received his B.A. and M.A. from the University of Chicago and his doctorate in architectural history at the University of Illinois at Chicago.

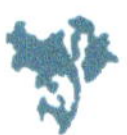

Mary Jane Jacob is a curator who holds the position of Professor and Executive Director of Exhibitions and Exhibition Studies at The School of the Art Institute of Chicago. As chief curator of the Museums of Contemporary Art in Chicago and Los Angeles, she staged some of the first U.S. shows of

American and European artists. Then shifting her workplace from the museum to the street, she critically engaged the discourse around public space with such landmark site-specific and community-based programs as "Culture in Action" in Chicago, and "Conversations at The Castle" during the Atlanta Olympics, and "Places with a Past" for the Spoleto Festival USA—which launched two decades of public engagement in Charleston, South Carolina. More recently her programs have led to co-edited anthologies: *Buddha Mind in Contemporary Art*, *Learning Mind: Experience into Art*, *The Studio Reader: On the Space of Artists*, and the forthcoming volume *Chicago Makes Modern: How Creative Minds Changed Society*. At the 2010 College Art Association Conference, Jacob was awarded the Women's Caucus for Art Lifetime Achievement Award and Public Art Dialogue's Lifetime Award for Achievement in the Field of Public Art; in 2011 she was honored by the women's leadership organization ArtTable as one of the key influential women in the field of visual arts in the U.S.

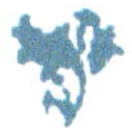

Lisa Junkin is an educator who works with diverse communities in Chicago. Since 2008, she has directed the education program at the Jane Addams Hull-House Museum, managing a staff of museum educators and coordinating public programs for children and adults. While completing a master's degree in Art Education at the School of the Art Institute of Chicago, Lisa worked at the Hyde Park Art Center as a teaching artist and public programs assistant. She also collaborated with high school youth on anti-violence and healthy relationship initiatives with the Lieutenant Governor's Office and After School Matters. Before moving to Chicago, Lisa interned and worked in Washington D.C. at the Corcoran Gallery of Art, The Phillips Collection, and the Hirshhorn Museum and Sculpture Garden. She is on the National Board of Editors for The Public Historian, a journal published by the National Council on Public History.

Research:

- printing optio
- price
- deadline

- 3D Scanning of
- holograms?

☆ Black envelopes → Napoleon Project

2-3 sentences & location on each planned piece title?

(by Saturday)

☆ medical people sende opening · email

For Future Surgeries:

- marionette type attachment
- nano surgeries in the brain (stimulate vs. white hat, simulate social challenge
- remote surgeries (maybe in multiples)
- surgeon as night watchman

Headache pills:

Skullcap, valerian, rosemary, chamomile, pe
equal parts powdered herbs, blend with honey

Mandrake, henbane, Datura metel, Datura i

Angelica dahurica
wolfsbane
Lingusticum wallichii or Szechuan Lova
Angelica sinensis or "female ginseng"
Chinese monkshood
Jimson weed
Mandragora officinarum
rhododendron flower
jasmine root

www.ingramcontent.com/pod-product-compliance
Ingram Content Group UK Ltd.
Pitfield, Milton Keynes, MK11 3LW, UK
UKHW062309290726
14090UKWH00018B/966